Thursday's child

Eartha Kitt

ILLUSTRATIONS

PART ONE

1

I WAS BORN in a little town called North in South Carolina.

The house I remember most was the last one I saw in the South as a child, that of the Stern Woman—at least that's what we called her. She was an elderly woman with dark complexion and gray hair. She had two grandchildren living with her—Gracie and Willie.

I don't remember how we came to live with them exactly but I do remember some things before that.

My first scene in life was a long dark dusty road. I could not see the end of it, for it just went down, down, down—to end in what to me seemed like hell. I hung onto my mother's hand as though life or death depended on it. My sister Pearl was in her arms. Mama began to hum as the sun sank into the ground ahead of us.

The wheat began to sway in the evening breeze and the cotton stood still and glared out at me with bulging eyes as we walked the narrow road through the fields.

I couldn't figure out why we were way out here so late or where we had come from or where we were going. I wanted to ask Mama, but I was afraid I would get her annoyed. Mama heaved a sigh as she adjusted Pearl in her arms. She looked down at me with wet eyes and stroked my long bushy brown hair. Something did not rest right in me—I felt as though I had done something and was going to get a whipping for it, but I couldn't remember what it was.

Then we saw the silhouette of a house in the distance.

"Mama, are we home?" I asked.

"No, baby, not yet," she answered.

"Mama, I want some water," I said.

"Yes, baby, I know," Mama said. Mama switched Pearl, grabbed me by my left hand, and quickened her pace.

"Uh, good evening," Mama said, as the woman opened the door. "Would you mind if I came in for a while to rest and give my children some water?"

The kind-faced woman opened the door wider and greeted Mama with a smile of complete comfort. "Come in, please," she said.

There was a fire burning in the fireplace and I headed for that. I sat down on the floor and began to wonder if Mama was going to stay here for the night or forever. I wanted to stay—I didn't want to go back out into the night. Spooks might be roaming around out there and take me away. The woman soon brought us some bread and clabber milk and a pan of hot soup. She and Mama mumbled a conversation as I dreamed in the firelight.

Soon I heard Mama thanking the woman for her kindness. She started to gather up my sister who was sleeping on the floor, wrapped in some old blankets. I realized we were ready to go wherever it was we were going, so I bundled myself up and followed Mama out the door into the darkness. As Mama said good-by and thanks I looked to see if any spirits were around or if the bogey man were watching from behind some old tree.

Again we walked. By this time the moon was bright and the trees along the way threw shadows. We began to edge the forest and I knew the bogey man would be in there if nowhere else—I saw a spirit behind every tree. I clung closer to Mama—

There was a spirit following us—how can I tell Mama? I have to scream—no, I can't—Mama, hold me in your arms like Pearl. I'm too scared to walk down here by myself. The feeling of loneliness crept over me as though I was being covered with a blanket.

After what seemed like years of walking with the spirits, Mama stopped. I could see her, tall and thin, like a pine tree, as she stood among the pines. She laid my sister down on the ground and looked around for me. I was there, glaring at her in wonderment.

Why did she stop, what did she lay Pearl down for—are we going to sleep here? Where is a house for us, where is our cow and our horse, where are our chickens and pigs? Where did we come from? Why? I never for a moment stopped trying to find the answer to why.

Mama began to arrange a bed of pine straw. When it was finished, she comforted Pearl. When she thought Pearl was sleepy enough, she turned and made a bed for me and one for herself. All this was done in a clump of small bushes to protect us from the dew. She covered us with pine and some old clothing we were carrying and lay down to rest.

I don't remember going to sleep. I was determined to stay awake until the sun came up. I cuddled closer to Mama. She had no idea how scared I was.

Let's see—if any spirit comes after us, I'll dig a hole and bury myself—no, that won't be quick enough. I'll hide behind that big pine tree—no, it can see me. I'll get on my knees and pray so that God will give me wings to fly away—no, God may not hear me.

It's a full moon, so maybe only the good spirits are roaming around tonight. Anyway, maybe if I pray hard enough, God will make me a spirit, too—then they can't bother me.

If I go to sleep, will Mama go off and leave me alone? Will she remember that I am with her too?

I woke up and saw Mama straightening her clothes out on her body. "You stay here and mind Pearl," she said softly. "I'll be back in a minute." As she walked away, she called back, "Don't go off anywhere, now. Stay right there."

I wondered why she left me and Pearl alone. Pearl was awake and playing with the pine straw. "Don't put that in your mouth, Pearl."

I wanted her to talk to me, but, being only one, she didn't make much sense. I thought she was awfully stupid.

I certainly hope Mama hurries up. I'm getting scared out here all by myself. I wonder how far we are from people? I could have found plums or blackberries or wild cherries or something for us to eat. What did she go for anyway? There isn't even a hickory nut tree near this old spot. When I grow up I won't be in any old pine-tree woods. I'm gonna sit in the shade and smoke my pipe all day and eat—just eat all the sideback, greens, cornbread, white bread, molasses and cream, sweet potatoes—all the eats I want. Pearl can have all the string beans and okra 'cause I don't like them.

Here comes Mama with an arm full of something. I hope she has something good. Wish there was a spring nearby—I'd go down and get me some water. Wonder what Mama has?

"There," said Mama, putting her load down beside us. "Watermelon, cantaloupe, and some fruit."

She must have stolen these things from someone's field because she was mighty dirty around the knees. Her hands looked as though she had been digging. Mama gave Pearl a little of everything, and, as she broke off pieces of fruit for me, I sank my teeth and fingers into them. We finished everything. Then Mama gathered us up again and started walking.

The next scene I remember was walking into the yard of a house that I seemingly knew before. Mama knocked at the door and a very pretty brown-skinned woman with long Indian hair came to greet us. The conversation between her and Mama was vague. I couldn't make out what was being said. Before we went in, I noticed lots of houses close together around—and the road was hard (paved, I learned later). This was a strange kind of place to me.

We went in. The room was very pretty, like the woman—a nice chair, a nice bed, a nice fireplace. It was cool inside. Mama rested Pearl on the floor and told me to mind her.

Pearl was awake and started to crawl around the floor. "Don't touch that, Pearl," I said, as Mama and the pretty woman went into another room. I lay down on my stomach on the floor and played with Pearl. I took her in my arms and petted her. She didn't want to be petted. She wanted the floor instead of me. She doesn't know any better. When she gets older, she'll love me, I betcha. I have to make her love me. Maybe if I rock her on my knee and sing her a baby song she'll like me. With this thought, I proceeded to rock the hell out of my little sister, who soon became so dizzy she laughed like a hyena and drooled all over me.

I didn't realize she could hardly breathe with me holding her so tight. Soon she began to gag for breath and slobbered more than ever. Then she let out a scream that the devil himself could hear, which made me drop her to the floor in surprise. Frightened, I stood stiff as a board as Mama and the pretty woman came running to see why I was murdering my poor little sister.

"What did you do to her?" Mama yelled. I stood in silence and gazed at Pearl on the floor and followed her limp body into the arms of Mama. "There, there," Mama comforted her. Was she really dying or was she coming back to life again?

What could I do to get so much attention? Maybe if I went into the yard to play, I would get out of Mama's way. "Ma-ma—" She didn't hear me. She finally had Pearl quiet. I opened the front door and walked cautiously out onto the porch. There was the nice rocking chair. It looked so all alone—

I went over to it and fondled it. Then I placed myself firmly into its seat, looking to the floor to see if my feet would touch. They didn't. I got out of the chair, started it to rocking with my hands, then jumped into it. The force of my body nearly toppled the chair over backwards. This scared me into taking it easy. I sat holding on with both hands and rocked back and forth. Soon I became tired and got out and sat on the step.

A moping dog came up. He turned and looked at me with such sad eyes, walking sideways around the house, that I hated myself and the world. I sat with my head in my hands and sulked.

The sun was going down as I thought of all the things I wanted to do and have. I watched the skies change colors. I loved the evening.

Mama and the pretty-faced woman were fixing something for dinner. I went into the sitting room to play with Pearl, but she was asleep. I sat down on the floor, gazed into the fire, and began to dream my usual dreams of nothing in particular—I would think myself out of this world into another where nothing much happened except I was happy. No one was around me in my dreams—I was always alone but some inner spirit kept me from wanting anything but that. To me there was nothing else—in my thoughts there were no tears, just laughter. My mother was not my mother but an angelic figure that hovered over me to guide me, to comfort me, to love me.

The next morning, we started on our march again. I don't recall all the details on the road, but I do remember the end of our journey came at my mother's uncle's house. I didn't know whose house it was when we reached it, but I felt as though I had been here before too.

We walked across a little bridge that connected two fields, belonging to the two uncles. A thin thread of water flowed in the stream. Across the stream stood an outhouse. Some chickens ran around the yard. The dogs began to bark, the pigs in their pen began to oink, the mules raised their heads in the stalls, the house was still, the children stared—and I was scared. Mama walked slowly into the yard, onto the porch, up to Uncle, who stood in the doorway watching her as though she was an evil creature.

I clung to Mama's dress, holding on to the hem for fear Mama would not win the battle. From the looks of Mama, she was scared too. Pearl, not knowing night from day, began to cry. All of our feelings were connected, it seemed.

Six or seven children stood in the yard at different angles—all looking, watching to see what our next move was to be.

The silence broke when Mama reached Uncle.

"What do you want?" he boomed out.

My mother replied meekly, "I have no place to stay. Would you please let me stay here for a few days until I find somewhere to go?"

"I've had this out with you before—the answer is the same, no!"

"Can't you see I've trudged from one place to another, trying, trying—I won't be a burden on you. I'll work, I'll earn my board and keep." Mama began to cry. "Just let me have some place to rest my children for a while." Mama looked at me; Uncle looked at me.

"She's no trouble, she's a good girl," Mama said.

"I don't care what she is, I—" Uncle roared.

"Please don't hurt her now," Mama sobbed.

Uncle stomped back into the house mumbling. Mama followed him, pleading. I stayed on the porch, wondering what the quarrel was about. I wanted to follow Mama but something told me to stay where I was. So I sat and waited. None of the children came near me. They went on with whatever they were doing, as though I did not exist.

One of the dogs came loping by. I thought he was going to welcome me, or at least try to get acquainted, but he just smelled my legs and went off. A cat came out of the window onto the porch. She mewed her way onto my lap and sat as though I was a long-lost friend. She showed me the only sign of friendliness.

For what seemed like hours, Mama stayed inside the house while I played with the comforting cat. I must have fallen asleep because, when I came to, the sun had gone down and Mama was pulling some raggedy covers over me and Pearl on the floor of a barn. There was hay on the floor and bales of cotton stacked in a corner. I could hear the sound of the night wind pushing its way through the cracks in the walls. I looked up at the spider-webbed ceiling and went back to sleep.

The next day I awoke at the call from Mama. She gave me a piece of bread and a cup of clabber milk. She gave the same to Pearl. Her face was worn. I thought she might have been crying but she looked at me and smiled. Her hands ran over my brown hair that needed combing. I wanted to ask her what was wrong but I didn't want to disturb her thoughts.

We must have been there for a couple of days when I heard her and Uncle through a window outside of the house, arguing.

"You gotta leave here," he said.

"I haven't found any place to go," Mama said.

"I don't care—but you can't stay here."

"I'm no trouble to you—"

"I don't want that yalla gal in my house. I told you that before—"

Yalla gal, yalla gal, yalla gal—the sound of the words played tricks on my mind. Yalla gal, yalla gal—

"'Don't bring your troubles to me. I have enough of my own, taking care of my children." Uncle went on and on. "That yalla man you went off with was no good to anyone. Nobody liked him but you. No one asked you to have a child by him."

Mama was crying now. I couldn't make out what she was saying.

I ran into the woods and cried all day until the sun went down. I wanted to run away but there was nowhere to go and I was too scared. As the sun slid behind the trees, I sneaked back to the house and hid underneath the porch until it was completely dark.

A few days later Mama came to me and Pearl with news that we were moving to another house. I was glad and sorry at the same time, because I wanted to leave this place, but I didn't know where we were going. We went along to a house that was a morning's walk from Uncle's house.

The house belonged to an elderly woman, who met us at the door. She knew Mama and was expecting us. She led us to our room which had two beds, one window, and a bedpan. The house was in pretty good shape as far as I could see. The living room had a fireplace, a few pieces of furniture, and two windows. There was another bedroom where the old woman slept. The kitchen was small and had a narrow hall leading into the yard.

Mama made Pearl and me comfortable and went off. The old woman sat around fingering some yardage in her hands. I was scared to go too near her for fear she would notice I was a different color than she was. Pearl had no fears and stayed near the old woman's feet all the time.

I learned later that the old woman was completely blind. Mama had arranged with the old woman that she would take care of the house, cook, tend to the fields, and everything if we could stay with her. Everything seemed to work out fine.

2

I soon made myself at home. I worked in the fields beside Mama when I could and when the sun wasn't too hot. When it was, Mama would leave Pearl and me at home. I could take care of Pearl, feed her, rock her to sleep, and laugh with her.

Later I made a playhouse at the edge of the woods. I cleaned a portion of the ground of pine straw and roped it in in three sections, a living room, a bedroom, and a kitchen. I gathered all kinds of old pots and pans and tin cans. I made rag dolls for my children, though very often I used my sister for my little girl. I had all kinds of rags and sacks and whatnots for my bedding and curtains.

I often stayed in this shaded spot for hours, sometimes all day in the peace and quiet, until Mama called me in to eat. Afterwards I would go right back to my make-believe world. A part of my playhouse was under a group of bushes. I would crawl under and hide from the showers when the weather was bad.

I used to play cook for my sister. I made mud pies and biscuits and all sorts of food fancies. Sometimes I would find the string rope broken. Probably by some animal or other that roamed at night. We were not accustomed to seeing many animals, except rabbits and squirrels. We saw snakes, too.

Then I remember the day came when my mother's attention was taken up by a man who seemed to have come out of nowhere. Suddenly he was there, and suddenly, after a couple of months of courting Mama, he was gone, and Mama with him.

He used to come to the house at evening time to sit around. He played with my sister in between the times he was smooching with my mother. I sat and watched the coochie-cooching he'd give my sister, the rocking of her on his knee, the baby talk that passed between them. Mama would smile at both of them and I would stare into the fire, wondering why he did not coochie-coo with me.

There was no me, as far as he was concerned. I knew he did not like me for some reason. I became insanely jealous over the fact that he had taken what little attention I had away from me. Mama began to notice me less and less, till finally one day Mama took Pearl and me over to another house with our little belongings. She didn't bother to explain anything to me but I had everything all figured out.

Mama was going away with this man and was going to give us away to this woman who had two grandchildren, Willie and Gracie, each in his early teens. The talk that I heard was that the man whom Mama was going to marry said he would accept Pearl but not me. Having eight children of his own, he couldn't afford to have a yalla gal around to create malice among them. Mama, in order not to separate us, gave both of us to the Stern Woman.

I don't remember exactly what my feeling was, other than that of loneliness. To learn that even Mama didn't want me was a blow to me through and through. I remember standing in the yard of the Stern Woman's house, watching Mama leave us behind as she walked arm in arm across the fields with the man. We didn't see Mama again for a long time.

Pearl and I had a share of one of the beds in the one bedroom with the girl. The boy, the grandfather, and the Stern Woman slept together. I never thought of the house or beds as being overcrowded because this was all very natural to me. I soon began to take my life in its stride—wake up with the rest of the family at daybreak, go out to the yard to fetch kindling for the stove so that the Stern Woman and the girl could cook breakfast. When breakfast was over, wash the dishes, while the rest of the household, excluding my sister, went into the fields to pick cotton. Clean the house, feed the pigs, let the cow out of pasture, let the chickens out of their coops, feed them.

Sweep the yard and watch the cow to see that it did not go near any poisonous wild berry trees. There were many of these near the swamp and one in the middle of the pasture. I never could figure out why no one chopped them down if they were poison to the animals. I had to watch my sister and the cow at the same time and remember to give the mule fodder at certain hours of the day and see that the hawks did not eat up the watermelons and keep the weeds from swallowing up the garden vegetables or the flowers in the yard.

This being a full-time job, I had very little if any time to play until Sundays, which I spent hiding under the house because most of the time visitors came over on the Sabbath and, in order for them not to make fun of me, I thought it better to stay out of everyone's sight.

I had a habit of sucking my tongue, doubling my tongue backwards and sucking, which gave me the greatest pleasure. As my mouth had to be slightly opened in order to do this it was very noticeable. No one paid much attention to me, so it was a long time before I got a slap on the face for doing this. The slaps did not cure the habit but started another, which was to hide behind the house and accompany the little pleasure I had found with another one. I would put my hand inside my breast and feel the little sign I had of being feminine. There was absolutely nothing there but I wanted there to be.

When I was finally caught at this, the Stern Woman gave me a whipping that only the devil could have put in her mind to do. Not only that, the devil himself must have held the whip, because I never forgot it. The blisters on my backside would not allow me to.

I remember the stories we used to hear about the dead coming back to life—and other stories.

When there is a young moon, don't sleep on your back because the hag will ride you. As a result, even the thought of sleeping on my back nerved me. I could never find a good solution for this tale except that, the beds being overcrowded, everyone had to sleep on his side to make room for others.

Don't walk over a broom or you'll spend your life in jail, or you won't get married.

Don't kill a bluebird—this means bad luck—and if a spider descends on a string of his web, don't let him rise again. This means death.

If anyone is lying down, don't step over him or you'll catch all of his sickness.

If you kill a snake, be sure you don't leave it lying on its back—it'll bring rain. Also, be sure it's dead, for if it isn't its mate will come and nurse it back to health.

Many of these superstitions I lived by and was conscious of in my every move, though secretly I would try to disprove them.

When the Stern Woman did not leave me and Pearl at home, she would take us into the fields, and I would pick cotton alongside her on the same row. Pearl was left at the beginning of each row, lying on a cotton sheet or on the cotton that was already picked. I got yelled at quite often because I would try to show speed rather than thoroughness, leaving half the cotton in the bulbs. The Stern Woman would make me come back and repick the same stalk. Once in a while the Stern Woman would leave us all home—the grandchildren, Pearl, and me—when a field was nearly finished and not everyone was needed. She would set duties for each of us to do by the time she came home.

These days were usually fun for the grandchildren. As soon as the elders left the house, the children began. The boy would get a peach-tree switch and begin to whip me around the legs in order to make me do his chores as well as mine. The girl would sit and laugh. I remember once the two grand-children tied me in a croaker sack, covering me to the waist. My hands were tied into the sack above my head. Then they tied me to a peach tree and stripped me of my skimpy panties so that I was bare. They proceeded to whip me for what must have been hours, until I cried for the earth to open and swallow me. They laughed and laughed, calling me yalla gal, yalla gal. The boy sat upon a limb, ate peaches, and threw the peach pits at me as hard as he could. When it was time for the elder members of the family to come home, they untied me and dared me to tell. If I did, they swore to do the same thing again first chance they got.

I was in fear of everything and everyone. I didn't want to make a false move, so everything I did was carefully done to get a smile from someone, anyone. I never said anything unless it was absolutely important or unless I was spoken to. I didn't even talk to Pearl very much, for they had turned her against me to the point where they had her lying to the Stern Woman and saying that I was eating sand. Every day for a period of what must have been three weeks, I got a whipping for the same thing—eating sand. It never occurred to the Stern Woman that the same story every day must have been a lie. As a result of getting so many whippings for something I was not guilty of, I decided one day to see what there was in eating sand.

I was absolutely alone in a road that was pure white sand. I stopped to play for a while in the silvery, soft ground. I remember the place distinctly. It was on the edge of the pine forest. On one side of the road we had a patch of watermelon. At the edge of the melon patch was an old well. As I sat in this spot of glowing sand, I picked up a handful of dirt and licked it out of my hands like sugar. It became damp with the saliva in my mouth and seeped its way down my throat like honey. I sat crumbled up on my knees in the softness and gloated in the discovery of a new and different pleasure. I could smell the rain and the wonderful dust that is in the air before a rainstorm.

A few days later, as my sister and I were playing in a ditch, I discovered an even newer pleasure, the taste of clay—red, yellow, purple, all the colors of the rainbow, all had that same rainy taste. Whenever I was alone, I would combine my secret feasts, and for dessert I'd suck my tongue and feel the middles of my breasts.

3

One evening the grandfather returned home from selling the cotton at the mills. Only God knows how he managed to find his way back home because he was sloppy drunk. When he stopped the wagon in the yard, he fell on the ground for dead. As the others ran over to pick him up in pieces, I ran for the package in the wagon, which was usually filled with goodies after this kind of a journey. There were usually cookies and candy and a loaf of white bread, but this time we found a new kind of fruit. We didn't know where to begin to eat it, whether we should eat the skin or the insides or both. It was yellow and long with little black spots on it. The smell was wonderful; it roamed all through the house and out into the yard.

We discovered how this strange piece of fruit should be eaten when the old man came to after a half a day's sickness. It was called banana, he told us, and only the inside was good to eat, but already we had eaten as much of the skin as we could.

I remember once the Stern Woman was sitting in the house with a group of other women. They were having a quilting party. My big daily chore was to watch the cow to see that she didn't go near the poisonous bushes or the lima beans on the garden fence.

The Stern Woman told me to fetch her a cup of water, which meant I had to go to the well for a bucket of fresh water. I left the cow within sight and she was groping along, minding her own business, nowhere near the garden or any of the poison bushes.

When I got back with the water, all the other ladies decided they wanted a cup too. I kept looking out of the window to see the cow. Suddenly I noted she was out of sight. I dared not say anything, but when I finally reached the last woman, I made a dash for the yard. She had found her way to the garden and was pulling away at the lima-bean vines.

I ran to her as fast as I could, to pull her away, but she was not for leaving. She had taken a great liking to the beans and continued to eat away. My heart was in my mouth. What can I do to get enough strength to pull her away? As I tugged on her chain, my knees became weak and the devil tickled my spine. I was too scared to cry for help because if the Stern Woman knew that the cow was eating the beans, I would get a whipping.

When I finally got the cow away from the garden, words of prayer came into my mouth. "Please, God, don't let anything be wrong with her. She's the only cow we've got. Besides, she just had a little baby and you can't have a baby without its mother. Please, God—help me."

As the cow took a few steps, she wobbled—and then began to foam around her mouth. "Please, God, help me." The cow suddenly went down on her two front legs, first one, then the other.

No one seemed to be in sight of the cow and me. I thanked God for this, because maybe I could pray hard enough to make her be herself again. Gradually, she went down on all fours, moaning, but not loud enough to be heard from the house. I went down on all fours with her, begging her to get up again. Then the little calf that was locked in the barn began to cry. The cow turned her head toward the sound of her calf and moaned.

Seeing there was no hope of getting her on her feet again, I called the Stern Woman. When she saw us both on the ground, she screamed and asked what had happened. I tried to explain in my fluttery voice.

The woman suddenly became calm and sent me into the house for baking soda. The baking soda was administered by the old woman, as the rest pried the cow's mouth open. The calf was screaming louder than ever. Shortly after the baking soda was given to her, the cow began to swell up. I knew this was the end of her. Probably the end of me too.

The Stern Woman sent me over the fields and through the woods to Bugs' house to fetch him. I ran as fast as I could, but Bugs was not at home.

On my way back, I saw another friend of the family hoeing a patch of land. I told him to come over to see if he could help us. By the time we both got back, the cow had grown three times its size. Everyone stood around. The cow's head had fallen to the ground and there was no hope. Shortly after, she began to gasp for breath and chokingly died.

My body had no feeling to it. I stood and stared at the cow. No more milk, no more butter, no more cream—and all because of me. The Stern Woman just looked at me with hate. I felt so helpless. Why did God have to do this? Is the Stern Woman going to whip me? If she is, why doesn't she do it and get it over with? But she just looked at me, as though to say, "There has been nothing but bad luck ever since I took you into my house."

When the old man came home, all of the men got together to dig a grave, out in the middle of the cotton field where no cotton had grown for a long time. After the cow was buried, I sat on her grave until the sun went down. My sister played beside me. Nature and all her likeness was silent.

After a couple of weeks I was my normal self again and went on with my daily chores. One day, after everyone had left for the fields, Pearl and I were left alone. The old man used to leave his tobacco and cigarette paper on the mantel-piece. This day my curiosity got the better of me and I decided to see what it was like to roll a cigarette, put fire to it, and eat the smoke. I imitated the old man's way of making a cigarette. I put fire to it and sucked as hard as I could. After a few tries I got a sick headache. I figured I must have been doing something wrong because the old man didn't get sick when he smoked. I decided to watch him more closely.

After a couple of days I had it all figured out and began to make a habit of smoking. Every day, as soon as everyone left the house, I went for my usual cigarette. I hid the tobacco and paper and matches under the house on a ledge. This went on for a long time.

The grandfather must have known that I had been stealing tobacco, but he said nothing to me, waiting to catch me in the act. One day when everyone came home earlier than I expected, he caught me. There I was, sitting under the house, smoking away, sending smoke signals out to all the world. I got a terrible whipping for this and afterwards was locked out of the house. Pearl and I had to stay in the yard from then on, whether we liked it or not.

My other vice was eating raw sweet potatoes. But this was soon discovered because the tar from the potatoes left a tell-tale black ring around my mouth. After this I took to the watermelon patch. I would steal at least one small watermelon a day.

The year the lightning burned away the cotton was a bad one. We relied on the forest more than ever to carry us through the winter. I never ate so much molasses and bread in my life as I did that year. For dessert we would have a piece of fried fat back.

Everything went wrong that year. Even the possums were scarce. The rabbits did not multiply rapidly enough, and there wasn't a fish to be found in the creeks. The rest of the crops failed and the trees did not bear enough fruit to be preserved. The sauerkraut we made from collard greens and cabbage did not turn sour. The sweet potatoes we banked in the ground rotted from the frost and we damned near starved to death. We must have got through that year with our prayers.

When I was old enough to go to school, I was given books, a writing pad, and sent off to a little old school in the yard of St. Peter's Church.

I don't remember the first day, but I must have been around six when I started. The school was crowded and there were not enough seats to go around. A lot of us sat on the floor. The teacher would walk around the room mumbling things we never understood. I learned how to read by listening to the other kids and to the grandchildren when they read their lessons at home. School days were during the times when there was no field work, which was about two months out of the year.

My school days were cut short because these months were during the winter and often I didn't have enough clothes. One day a big box was sent to Pearl and me from up North. The box contained clothes and shoes. I suddenly became aware of the woman who sent us these things. I learned she was my aunt, who had gotten angry with my mother for marrying a man my aunt did not like. She had vowed she would not bother with Mama or us anymore. When she finally heard that my mother had just about abandoned us, she decided to send us as much as she could, when she could.

One Easter Pearl and I received beautiful things. My dress was white chiffon with little ribbons on the sleeves and neck. There were tiny little flowers sewn all over it, with a white slip to match. There were little white slippers and socks—with a tiny bonnet. My sister's dress was pink chiffon made exactly like mine. She too had a bonnet.

We both went to church, the envy of everyone who saw us. I was very proud of my costume and also of my sister. We even had little parasols to shade us from the sun.

The Stern Woman had Pearl and me get up in church and sing a duet, just so we would be shown off properly. As we sang, accompanied by a piano, the church rocked. with the people being moved by our wonderful spirit. This Easter Sunday was the most joyous of my life. It was the first time anyone and everyone paid so much attention to me. Our dresses were the topic of the day and my aunt became famous in about four hours.

I learned that she ran away from the South and went up North. She was my mother's sister who hadn't been seen for years. She was living in New York and was very rich. I took a great interest, wondering what she was like and would she send for me one day. Whenever I could, I would hide within hearing distance to learn more about this good woman up North.

One day my sister and I were sitting in the yard playing when we heard the chanting of the chain gang, building a new road near our house. We sat and listened, humming along with them when it was a familiar song. The chain gang was a natural thing, so no one paid much attention until one of the men, with chained feet, came riding a horse into the yard. He had a pail and asked for water from our well. He was very dark and wore a torn sun hat. He looked at us with eyes that envied our freedom. His shoulders were broad and strong. His chest and arms were muscled. His trousers were dirty and worn. The stripes were faded, so that it was hard to tell which were supposed to be black and which white.

He slumped over to take the water the old man gave him, turned his horse around, and headed back. As he reached the road that led back to the others, he swiftly turned his horse and headed for an opposite trail. He took off like a bat out of hell. Everyone in the house, my sister, and I sprang up to watch as he galloped off. The guards soon caught up with him. The ringing of their rifles reached our ears with a deathlike tone. We all bowed our heads and went back to our affairs, as if this too was all very natural.

We often heard the songs of the chain-gang criers, and voices of the callers that led the work. Often my sister and I sat on the edge of the road where they were working and watched for hours as they dug the soil and uprooted the tree trunks. The movement of their black bodies swaying to the sound of an ax or a pick and a grunt made me conscious of my chainless feet, my arms, my useful hands, the sand that hugged my feet. I became conscious of the sun that beat my body, the water that cooled. I became conscious of the desire to stay alive, to want to live.

I spent many hours in the pine woods gathering pine cones. I would lie in a sunny spot and think of the Heavenly Father. I would watch the few planes that passed overhead, wondering where they were going, where they had come from, what made them fly, and if there was a little man inside to make them run.

I watched the birds build their nests and feed their young. I watched the squirrels seek food and run from danger. I ate hickory nuts, wild plums, blackberries, and sipped water from the running brook. I picked daisies and threw love-me-nots to the wind.

This was all very natural. I longed for my mother but was never aware of my father. There was talk that he was killed shortly after my mother ran off with him, but no one ever gave me the real story, and I gave little or no thought to him.

I was happy when I was alone. I lived in my thoughts and when my thoughts and serenity were broken, I felt hate, unless Nature did it. She felt everything I felt and pitied me. To her I could talk and give all that I wanted to give. When it rained, I loved the rain—to run in it, to soak my feet in it, to wet my bushy brown hair in it, though I could never get it dry again. I belonged to Nature and Nature belonged to me.

The thunder would shake me inside. I would quiver to its rhythm. The lightning would light up my heart and I would want, with it, to lift something and be destructive.

My chores became easier for me as I grew older. My mind was aware of everything but only Nature was aware of me. One day news came to us that my mother had had a baby, a little girl. I became very jealous of this new baby. Mama hadn't been to see us for a long time; now she would never come, with someone else to keep her away.

Pearl and I were taken over to see the new baby—and I hated her more because she was like my sister in complexion, so I knew she would hate me, too, as soon as she grew old enough. She even resembled Mama a little.

Mama was considered a beauty, with jet black hair, brown complexion, big black eyes—and an Indian face. She was a beauty—even her stepdaughters were jealous of her. It was the talk of the county.

This jealousy soon became dangerous. Mama took deathly ill about six months after the baby was born. I was sweeping up the yard, with Pearl lagging around me, when a neighbor came to see the Stern Woman to tell her of Mama's illness. Everyone seemed concerned. It was all very mysterious.

The Stern Woman put on a shawl, as it was getting to be evening, said she would return as soon as she could, and left with the neighbor. She returned late that night and sat for hours in the living room in front of the fireplace, telling her husband of Mama's sickness. As the story went, Mama had suddenly become very sick after eating dinner one night, a plate of food sprinkled with what looked like red pepper. When Mama inquired about it, she was told that it was a new seasoning. When the dinner was eaten, Mama went to the living room to build a fire in the fireplace. She collapsed at the door and was caught by her husband who was just coming in the front door. He put Mama to bed and went off to town to fetch a doctor, who did not arrive until the following day. After the examination, the doctor said there was nothing he could do.

As I lay in bed, I listened intently to the strange tale being told by the Stern Woman, not understanding why Mama had taken so ill. She was so young and lively. She was strong and powerful and loved everyone. Everyone loved her. Tears began to wet the bumpy pillow. I wanted to wake Pearl, who was sleeping beside me, but I didn't want to make her unhappy.

We were told about Mama the next day, but we were not allowed to go and see her for the first couple of weeks. She was having fits of convulsions, they told us. One night she would wake up screaming, another night she would get up and walk the house as though there was nothing wrong with her at all. There were times when she would ask someone to comb her hair—she wanted to look pretty for St. Peter. At other times she would just lie there and stare at the ceiling.

Whenever anyone came to the house, I would find a hiding place to hear the latest news of my mother. I spent most of my time praying that she would get well. Whenever I went to the woodpile, I would pray as I knelt to pick up the kindling. No one knew how much information I had.

One day a man came to get the Stern Woman in his wagon. They went to my mother's house, I learned later. The grandson and the old man sat in the living room by the fire, waiting for the Stern Woman to return. I twisted and turned in my bed, knowing something was wrong. I tried to stay awake, but dozed off.

I was awakened by voices made by the house. It seemed that the back door flew open when the Stern Woman and the neighbors walked in the front door. The old man and his grandson swore that they had locked it earlier in the night. The story was that Mama had tried to reach us before the Stern Woman and the neighbors to tell us that she was dead.

When I heard the words, I felt Mama's presence in the room, hovering over the bed that held my sister and me. I could not cry until the words reached the center of my body and crawled to my feet. My hands became damp and cold. I wanted to wake Pearl but they might hear me and know that I had been listening. Soon we were called and told we no longer had a mother.

The next day we were taken over to see her laid out. They had put her on a slab and covered her with a sheet. Her hair was neatly combed. Her mouth carved a smile and her eyes seemed to shine through closed lids as though she was looking at me. I stood looking at her for a long time before I moved. Then we were taken into the living room, among conversations of Mama. They looked at me and said, "Look at Eartha, she knows what's going on." I had known what was going on for a long time.

A few days later Mama was buried in the graveyard of St. Peter's Church, beside the grave of her mother and dad. As her casket of wood slid to the bottom of the grave on ropes, I didn't cry at all. I just stared and wondered if my mother were going to heaven or hell. The sun was bright in its glare, and this was a good sign. God bless the child the sun shines on. After the dirt was carefully packed over the pine box and the Bowers were strewn about, my baby sister was passed over the grave so that my mother would not come back to claim her. Everyone went home, to continue life as it was. So did we, without Mama.

After the funeral, the house was torn apart, including the mattress of death. In each corner of the padding was an object of voodoo. Knotted together mysteriously were claws of animals, teeth of snakes, tails of weird things mixed with powders of swamp herbs. Letters swearing death were tied in a neat bundle at the center of the bed. This was supposedly done to keep her in agony to obtain the desire of death. In case one method failed, the other would win.

There was little for me to hope for any more, except that the good woman up North would continue to send Pearl and me clothes. I thought about her often.

4

The one community store was three miles away from where we lived and, to fetch store food or medicine, one had to walk. One night, sometime after Mama died, the Stern Woman took ill and needed some kind of medicine. She looked at her two grandchildren and asked them to go to the store. One looked at the other and moaned about the young moon and the darkness. Each was more frightened than the other to go out into the black night. The old man was sucking a bottle in the corner and was in no condition to do anything.

When I saw how sick the woman was, I said, "I'll go." They all looked at me in cold surprise. I was given some small change and was sent out. The night was blacker than ever and grew even blacker as the door was closed behind me. I followed the path leading through the fields into the forest of pines, judging every step carefully. If anyone was afraid of the dark, I was. I clenched my fists.

Finally I came to the end of the forest. In front of me was St. Peter's Church, the graveyard where my mother lay, and the school. A fork of the path led along a field and bypassed the church. To go forward meant going through the graveyard, but this path was quicker—besides, my mother would protect me.

I marched forward, step by step by step. I visualized the spirits sitting on the graves, cheering me on or trying to turn me back. Straight forward I went. I had to be sure the ground I walked on was solid, because some of the graves were soft dirt. If I stepped on one, I might sink into the ground, never to return. The sweat drenched my body, my feet were musty and held the dirt. My toes collected all the stones, my calves began to ache, and my heart stopped beating. At last I reached the end of the graveyard. A path continued through the fields.

When I walked into the store after knocking a long time for someone to open it, the white man was surprised to see me, my head barely reaching the top of the counter. "My, my, what are you doing roaming around in all this darkness?"

I made a grin, asked for the medicine, and left, running as fast as I could. I must have run all the way home with a little more courage. Now they will have more attention for me, I thought. I have shown them that I am not afraid of the dark. Maybe the Stern Woman won't beat me anymore.

When I gave the Stern Woman her medicine, she gave me a broad smile. I was like a puppy being patted on the head by its master. This was all I wanted. I went back into my little corner by the fireplace and watched the faces of the older ones pouting. The next morning the Stern Woman was much better. I was the first one to receive the breakfast she passed around the table.

Pearl and I used to have contests eating. We would sit on the step of the house backwards, with our feet hanging between two steps. "The one that finishes first helps the other." I would always let my sister win. I adored her. Whenever anyone came to the house, they would say, "What a good little girl," "What a pretty little girl." Her skin was brown and smooth. Her hair was very short, and she looked like a little boy. Her childish figure was perfect. I wished that I was like her. I forgave her for the hurts she caused me because she didn't know any better. Besides, she was my sister, and Mama wouldn't like it if I didn't like my sister. We were taught by her to love each other.

One time I was on my way to school. I had on high-button shoes and a croaker-sack dress. When I was nearing the school-house, a bunch of white kids came running toward me—with outstretched arms locked together. They yelled at me, "Get in the ditch, you son of a bitch. You ain't got no business on the road going to school.

You niggers got no business getting educated. You belong in the cotton fields."

I could hear the cotton fields calling me as I scrambled to get on my feet, after being shoved into the ditch. They went on down the road, laughing over the good job they had done to dirty my croaker-sack dress and hurt my feelings. I was too hurt to cry, and too mad and frightened to fight back. I went on to school, late. The teacher met me at the door with a ruler in his hand. As I walked past him, he made me open my hands and smacked the ruler in my palms. I refused to cry. I went and sat in my place in the classroom, hot all over. I was hurt, truly hurt.

One Saturday the Stern Woman sent the two grandchildren and me to work on a piece of land to be finished. Cotton at that time was a penny a pound. She told us to see how much we could pick in a half a day. I was happy to be put to the test. At the end of the morning, the white man came to weigh our work. The two grandchildren had picked one hundred and twenty-five pounds between them. Me, I had picked one hundred pounds all by myself. I was the happiest kid alive. To know I had earned a whole dollar. I glorified in my glory. I couldn't wait to get home to tell the Stern Woman.

As I walked home through the fields, lagging behind the rest, the plantation owners drove by in the wagon. One of them threw me some pecan nuts. This made me very happy. Everything was going well this day.

When we got home, the Stern Woman smiled at me and told me I was a good child to have worked so hard. She let me keep the dollar, and I guarded it with my life.

I had all kinds of plans for my dollar—I could buy a new dress for myself, I would buy some bananas, I would buy something for Pearl and me too. Maybe I could work every Saturday and make lots of dollars and get rich and buy a house with a porch and sit in the sun, eating bananas all day.

One morning I woke up with my eyes tight shut. I couldn't open them for the life of me. Later in the day, I could open them a little. I was miserable. When I went into the field alone, I looked into the sun, in hopes that this would cure my eyes, but it only made them worse. No one cared about my eyes, it seemed, as I walked around the yard half blind.

I stayed like this for a long time, continuing to look to the sun for help. I never found out what caused it, and no one bothered to tell me what it was, but I was damn glad when it got better.

I remember a dream I had. My mother walked into our yard out of the beams of the sun. She was more beautiful than ever. She smiled more than I had ever seen her smile. Pearl and I were sitting on the porch as she walked up to us, took us by the hand, and walked back to heaven through the rays of the sun.

I remember another dream I had: I was standing in the yard, looking at the rosebushes. When I turned my eyes to heaven I saw a cross of roses in all colors across the skies, with Christ's body clinging to it, like the picture I had seen of Him hanging on the Cross. His hands showed the nails that were pounded in them to hold Him fast. His feet were crossed, and a nail held them in place. The heavens were in brilliant colors of the rainbow, and they pointed to Him in striplike form.

5

All of a sudden my aunt sent for me. A box of clothing, accompanied by a letter and a train ticket, arrived one afternoon. Everyone gathered around to see what the box contained. There were three pairs of long underwear, three pairs of long cotton stockings, three undershirts, three petticoats, a pair of gloves, a beret hat, a pair of shoes, a scarf, one woolen dress, and one snowsuit jacket, some things for my sister, and a few other doodads.

The letter explained how to go about packing me off and putting me on the train. The letter said my aunt would be at the station to meet me, and told me what she would look like. The letter went on to say that she would send for Pearl as soon as she was able to, and for her not to worry.

For several days, until the day came for me to leave, I thought of nothing but going up North to be with the good woman. I did all my work with my heart in my mouth. I began to imagine what up North would look like.

Then they began to talk to me. "What do you want to go up North for? It gets so cold up there, people freeze to death." "The buildings are so tall, they sometimes collapse and tumble down on you." "The trains ride in the air and are always falling down on the ground." "People live on top of each other. You never have enough room to move around in." "You don't know when you are well off." "Why don't you tell her you don't want to come?"

I didn't say anything at all, but was determined to go, now that I had the chance. Pearl was very unhappy when I left, and started to cry when the man with the car came to take us to Orangeburg.

They had washed me in a tub of hot water, combed my hair, and made me clean as a whistle. All this was done in front of the fireplace, and I was as happy as a bluebird because I was going away—never to come back.

They braided my hair in three sections—two braids in the back and one down the side of my face. My hair was long and heavy, and I was very proud of it, until they put my hat on. My hair was so thick it took a long time for them to know what to do with the beret. Finally it was squeezed on, but I wouldn't let on that it was hurting my head. I suffered gladly.

They made me a box of catfish sandwiches on white bread. The first time in my life I had all the store white bread I wanted, as well as a piece of sweet potato pie and some wild plums. This was for me to eat on the train.

We all piled in the car and were off to Orangeburg. Everyone kept telling me how miserable I was going to be up North and that I would beg to come back. I turned off my listening.

When we arrived, the Stern Woman talked to the station-master about me, and he put a tag on me with my name on it, saying who was going to meet me and where I was going and where I was coming from. I stood on the platform, with my eyes down the tracks to see when the train was coming. I said nothing to anyone, not even Pearl. I didn't hear anything or see anything until I saw the train finally chugging its way to me. With a huff and a puff, it growled into the station.

No one got off, but people got on. Seemed like everyone and his brother was going where I was going, up North. A porter came out and stood by the train with a pair of steps. He helped me on with a broad smile. "Where are you going, little girl?" he asked.

"I'm going to New York," I answered boldly. My seven years were firm in my mind. I was grown, fully grown. I went and sat down in a seat next to a window, followed by the rest of them, talking to me. The porter came and assured the Stern Woman that he would look after me.

Finally the train in a huff of smoke was moving away. I sat still in my seat, looking out of the window, saying good-by in my mind. I saw the fading figures of Pearl and the rest, waving at the train, and I remembered I had not said good-by to them.

My face held no sign of a smile. My body was calm with excitement. My mouth tightened with expectation, the hair on my head stood still and my breath quickened. I was off to the North.

I gazed out of the window all night, without a wink of sleep. When I got hungry, I ate my catfish sandwiches. I was aware of every stop and every little town, of every road and light, of every car and field, of everybody and everything that came in sight. The chugalug of the train brought nearer a new world and a new life and the good woman. I looked at no one on the train and talked to no one.

The porter would pass once in a while to see if I was all right. He would smile and go on his way. Through the night, I tried to imagine what my aunt would look like. Since I couldn't I soon put her out of my mind, except for a shadow that lingered in back of my head. Will she like me? was carried in rhythm by the tracking of the train.

My forehead was glued to the window in between my catfish sandwiches and sweet potato pie.

Then, out of the blackness, the train zoomed into grayness, with a little color here and there. I could see the sun faintly eyeing its way over a hilltop. Then it got lighter and lighter and the colors got brighter and brighter and soon it was the full light of day.

The porter came to me and said we were almost in New York. He put my little suitcase my aunt had sent me and my shoebox of food on the seat beside me. As soon as this was done, my eyes were back at the window.

The train slowed down and began to tease me. I kept thinking, if this thing had a horse to it, it would go faster than this. Will she be there? Maybe she forgot I'm coming. Maybe they just sent me off to get rid of me. What'll I do if she doesn't find me? When the train finally stopped at the station and the porter came to get me, he had to pull me away from the window.

I was gazing at the people, running to and fro. They reminded me of cattle being pushed into a pen. I had never seen so many people at one time in my life. When I got outside of the train, a tall brown-skin woman walked up to me with ease. She had a smile on her face that made me smile. She really wanted to laugh, I felt, but didn't want to hurt my feelings. She said, "Eartha Mae?"

"Yesseum." I looked up at her. She stood about three times my size. She bent over to look at my tag, to see if I was really who I said I was. "So this is what you look like?"

Through my mind went the same thought. She took me by the hand and led me through the hustle and bustle of an ant den. She had to drag me along, for my eyes were bewildered at the sight of things.

Where could all of these people be going, and why? Why do they all huddle in one place? People were greeting each other, saying good-by to each other, scuddling with bags—and pushing—running and walking—standing and chatting—I was just numb.

The good woman pulled me along, until we upped a pair of stairs that never ended, and finally were outside on the street. This was where I stopped breathing and became a statue. I stood with my head bent back, trying to look at the tall buildings. I became nervous, for surely any minute one of them was going to topple over on me.

My aunt was patient and allowed me to absorb as much as I could in my first few minutes of surprise. She was able finally to drag me on a bus that stopped under a steel road that a train traveled on in the air. The bus was very crowded, but my aunt managed to get us a seat in the back of it, where in between chuckles she tried to adjust my beret. After she adjusted as much as she could, I kneeled on the seat and looked out the bus window.

We arrived safely at her place on West One Hundred Forty-third Street, where we mounted two flights of stairs. I remember entering the apartment, met by one of the girls who lived in the house. It belonged to a family of five named Wayde. My aunt rented a room with them.

They took me into the living room, where we all got acquainted except for the boy and little girl about my age, who were in school.

Someone turned on a light that immediately got my attention. I looked at the light for a long time, wondering how it went on and why. I went over to the button and fiddled with it until I made the light go out again. I switched it on and off until I was stopped.

Soon my aunt took me into another room and began to undress me. She got hysterical with every piece she took off. My coat and hat, my dress, my three slips, three underwear, three pairs of long panties, three pairs of stockings, and my shoes. She called in the rest of them to laugh, too. Every stitch of clothing she had sent had been put on my back.

I went through the house when they finished with me and had put me in something more comfortable, turning on the lights and turning them off. I soon discovered the gas stove that lit up when you turned a knob and went out at the twist of a wrist.

Then I discovered the radio that someone turned on later in the day. I couldn't figure out why it talked or played music or made human sounds. I kept turning the radio on and off, on and off.

Suddenly I had to go to the little girl's room. I looked out of the glassed window into a yard of concrete. There was no outhouse.

Where does one go? It must be downstairs somewhere, but how will I find it? I had to give in and ask my aunt. She took me to a tiny little room and closed the door.

I looked at the different things in the room and tried to figure them out. I managed to turn on the water in a bowl. I played around with the knobs in the big tub; that couldn't be it. Finally I called my aunt. She came in and showed me the proper bowl; laughing, she went out, closing the door.

Later I took my place in front of the window that looked onto a street and waited for the little girl who I was told was about my age. It was nearly time for her to be coming home from school. As the hour drew nearer, I noticed there were more and more children, yelling and playing. Then I noticed a little girl walking alone. This must be her, I thought. When the doorbell rang a few moments later, I knew I was right. She came into the room where I was, and we soon became pals.

After a few weeks, my aunt took me to be registered in school. This was the most frightening thing of my life. I remember having a needle prick my arm. My arm swelled up and I was sickly. I was taken to a classroom of children much smaller than I was. My aunt talked to the teacher, whose name was Miss Beans, and I was placed in a seat among snickering children. The teacher explained to the class that I had just come up from the South and must start my schooling from the beginning. My class was 1A.

No one tried to get acquainted with me, and I didn't know how to go about getting to know anyone. My aunt brought me to school every morning, came at the lunch hour to sit with me, and came to fetch me home after school for the first couple of weeks, until I knew my way to and fro. After that, she made arrangements for me to get my lunch in school.

I didn't have too much trouble because I stayed away from everyone. Those who tried to pick a fight soon stopped, because I just wouldn't lift my arms to fight nor would I answer back. I must have been in school for at least six or eight weeks before I got into my first fight. A girl pushed me down and I hurt my knee. As I was tending to it, I was hit on my behind, to the laughter of everyone who watched. I was forced to fight. My arms went out but I couldn't get angry for some reason. I became nervous and started to cry, even though I was not hurt much. I didn't want to hurt her, so I took all the blows. The more she hit me, the less I cried. Someone soon broke the fight up. The school bell rang and we all went to our classes, me with my hurt feelings and they in their fearful joy. No one said anything to the teacher about it.

Soon it got around the school that I was a coward, and everyone began picking on me. I wanted to tell my aunt, but I knew I had to figure it out myself. There was tension in me every noon when school broke for lunch.

One day this bully girl came up to me with her gang and started a conversation. They asked me questions and I answered. All the kids egged her on. I had the feeling that everyone was afraid of her. She told me she was going to beat me up if she caught me after school. Everyone walked away laughing. I sat frozen in my seat that afternoon, waiting until three o'clock for the bell to ring.

Should I ask the teacher to let me leave earlier or should I try to fight? I was too scared to ask to leave, and I was too scared to stay. I walked out of the school on pins and needles. None of the gang was around, but, as I got to the corner, out of the candy store came the girl and all her little boosters. She walked up to me and said, "I told you you'd better not let me catch you. Why don't you run? Go ahead, run!"

The thought came to my mind that either I stood my ground or they would laugh at me more.

"Ain't you gonna run?" I stood my ground. They became nervous—I was nervous. "Why don't you beat her up and get it over with?" someone said. "She's gotta hit first," another said. "She ain't gonna move. Hit her!"

Then suddenly the girl came toward me. Someone had pushed her. My hands went out and she went to the ground. This brought cheers from the crowd. "She knocked her down, she knocked her down!"

This encouraged me. I stood with my fists tight, waiting for a blow to get me angry. The girl got up in fury. We went at each other like tigresses. I finally downed the girl, who went off with a bloody nose and torn clothes. She didn't show up at school the next day, and everyone sang my praise.

I gradually became a school favorite, not because of my fighting ability but because of my speaking abilities. Whenever my teacher asked me to read, the class would become silent. This was frightening because you could hear a pin drop. Though I loved to read, I was embarrassed. I would take my book, go to the head of the class, and read four or five paragraphs before the teacher would stop me. It was like a spell over the room. I didn't understand it at all, but it seemed I had some power that made people pay attention. I was proud of this and was willing to go on reading forever.

After a year in this school, I had done two years' work and had caught up with my age group. The assembly was successful for my class, it seemed, whenever I had anything in it. The longer my speeches were, the more successful I was. After a few assemblies, I caught on very quickly, and by this time had lost my Southern accent—that is, if I ever had one. I don't remember ever talking that way.

6

About my second year in public school, my aunt and I moved to another place to live with a man and his wife who were very nice. I think we had to move because the little girl and I had a lot of fights together, either because she took my doll, the only one I had, and broke it, or I took hers, or she started to wear my clothes. Then, too, the mother of the house complained that my aunt was not paying enough attention to me. My aunt would go off to work in the morning and I wouldn't see her again until night, maybe at dinner, maybe not. The family would see that I ate and was put to bed and went off to school in the morning.

At our new place, I could get up in the mornings by myself and prepare myself for school. When there was anything to eat for breakfast, I would eat; if there was nothing, I would go to school hungry. I could never understand when I couldn't find food, because I knew my aunt was working, or at least I thought she was working. My clothes became shabbier and shabbier.

I was soon aware of "relief." The word relief I never understood, but it gave me a feeling that someone somewhere was looking out for us. The meaning of relief was food, a dress, and apples.

One day my aunt sent me to collect what was due us that month. She called me upstairs from my play and told me the address of the relief station. She said, "Bring back as much as you can."

The station was on the last avenue of the East side and we lived on the last avenue of the West side. When I got to the station, the smiling man looked at me and said, "You can have two ten-pound bags, but you're too little to carry all that, so you better take one."

I said, "I can do it," remembering that my aunt had said, "Bring back as much as you can." In each arm I took a bag that was almost the size of me and walked out. The bags of apples were not heavy at first, but after two blocks one arm began to feel the strain. Then after another block, the other arm began to feel it. I put both bags down on a stoop and rested for a while. After I got my strength together, I took them both up with a struggle and continued my journey. Soon my whole body became strained, but this time I was determined not to stop. Then my legs gave way. I've got to get these apples home—I will not give up.

As I walked along, tears came to my eyes. The more apples I take home, the more I will have to eat. My aunt will make apple pie, applesauce, apple dumplings, stewed apples, apple cake, apple salad, or just plain apples. When I finally got home, worn to aches, my aunt laughed until she couldn't laugh any more. She said, "I didn't tell you to bring the whole relief station!"

As a reward, I thought she would make all the things I had thought of, but she never got beyond applesauce. I had just plain apples for weeks, but I was grateful because, as long as there was an apple in the house, I never got hungry.

I hated relief dresses, but wore them because they were better than the ones I had. Everyone in school who had on a relief dress was known and snickered at. I began to wonder why we were getting food and clothing from the city and who was so kind to do this.

I heard of a thing called WPA. What this meant exactly I didn't know. Everywhere I saw "WPA project." Men were busy working away on streets or buildings. What is the WPA? Or who is WPA? We began to learn about the government, and we had to know who the president of the United States was. Soon I learned that relief, WPA and love were all one and the same—President Roosevelt.

He became alive in my mind, like God was alive, like my aunt was alive, like people were alive. He became my friend and in my mind a friend of all people who wanted to eat, be warm, and work. Everywhere I went, I was conscious of the president of the United States and I was grateful, because I felt he was aware of me.

My aunt had always been a great church woman, so she expected me to be a great churchgoer. I had joined the Methodist church and was a member in good standing for a long time. I was a member of the children's choir and went to Sunday school every Sunday. I was chosen for church recitals and talks, and I was starred in the church plays.

The children's choir consisted of about eight girls and six boys. I was selected to lead the singing. After the singing there were sounds of "Amen!" and "Hallelujah," until the preacher got up to give the sermon. Sometimes the singing and preaching and hallelujahs went so well that everyone was shouting and jumping up and down. I loved these times—the love of God swept through the church. I would get warm all over. People would cry and hum—sing and pray.

The more plays I did in church and school, the more the word would get to my aunt that I was a great little actress. "You must encourage her," they would say. The more they would say it, the more I expected my aunt to encourage me, but the more I expected it, the less encouragement I got. That is to say, none, absolutely none at all. When my aunt came to the church to see me in a play, I would try to glance at her from the stage, but most of the time she would sit in the back so that I could not see her. When the play was over, she would come to take me home. As we left people would tell her how wonderful I was. She would say, "Thank you." Then she would take me home in silence, never saying if she thought I was good or not. Sometimes I would try to take her hand, to show her that I loved her and for her to show me likewise. But she would somehow manage to miss my hand.

I was taking piano lessons, which I hated, but it was to please my aunt and I was determined to please her. I took lessons every Tuesday and Saturday faithfully, but it was hell to get me to practice. My teacher, knowing this, would make me practice before and after my class. This way I was gradually becoming fairly good.

When my aunt was home, I would play the things I liked, and this was easy. Most of them were learned photographically—looking at the paper once or twice I could play just about note for note whatever was on the page, providing it was easy. If it was too much work, I would put it aside until I had to learn it. Then when I did, no one could stop me from playing it.

When I got to my next to last year in junior high school, through the encouragement of my teacher, Mrs. Bishop, I graduated a year ahead of my time for high school. This meant I could take an oral test for a special school to study dramatics, the New York School of Performing Arts. When Mrs. Bishop asked me if I would be interested, I was very pleased, but, when she told me what I had to do, I almost gave up the idea. It meant being tested before a group of people, which to me was more frightening than anything I had gone through in my life. Suppose I did not win—suppose they did not like me?

"Well," said Mrs. Bishop, "I'll make an arrangement with the teacher of that school to have you go down and get acquainted with her. After you meet each other, if you want to go through with it, fine. It's up to you." She didn't quite convince me. Then she said, "No one has to know about it but us. If you don't pass, that's that. You'll continue on here. No one will be the wiser."

The teacher of the new school and I met and got along well. She told me what was expected and asked me to prepare a speech to be read aloud in front of a group of students and faculty members.

A few weeks later, I went back to the school, but when I was called on to recite, I was frozen with nervousness. As I started, the room became still, and more still. I felt as though I was talking in a vacuum, with no one around. I felt as though I was in a glass cage with no sound except that of my own voice. Then my voice had no sound. It was as though my mouth just formed words but no sound.

The faces looking at me were no longer faces but masks staring into space.

But I had done what I had hoped to do, gained control of those in the room. My body held an electric feeling of satisfaction, giving me the knowledge that I had won them. When I sat down, my teacher, who was really my teacher after that because she encouraged me more than anyone to go into the theater, sat at her desk with great pleasure in her eyes and face. I looked at her with tears and warmth in my heart because I knew we would become great friends.

The students were asked to explain what there was about me that they did not like. No one had anything to say. As the class broke up, the students left the room, looking back at me. One or two came over and smiled. One said, "See you when the term begins."

I was in. . . .

7

When I went into high school, my aunt had moved to a neighborhood that was strange to me. These people spoke a language I did not understand—most called it Cuban, though some called it Puerto Rican.

There was a man living with us, or we were living with him—I never could figure out which was which. He had a key and came and went as he pleased. There was one bedroom, a living room, kitchen, and bath. When I did not sleep with my aunt, I slept on the couch in the living room.

Being about fourteen years old, I began to notice the boys and the boys began to notice me. I wanted often to invite them to come up and meet my aunt, but she suddenly turned against boys and told me not to speak to them. I became very curious about this and wondered why. I would stand on the stoop of the house, afraid to talk to anyone who passed by or who tried to talk to me.

Everyone, it seemed, spoke this different tongue. I listened carefully. I would hear one word more than once—this one I would remember; then I would pick out another to remember. When I asked about them later, I learned that some of them were not so decent.

I began to make friends with the girls in the block and go around with them. They would meet boys in the evenings and sit on the stoops and chatter away. I had to learn what they were saying, but I didn't want to let them know I had no idea what they were talking about. Now and then an English phrase would be heard. From this I could get a notion of the conversation. As I became more curious, I gained more friends, and bit by bit I was able to understand more. Soon I could pick up a conversation in no time.

Without my aunt's knowledge, I was seeing boys more than she imagined. Whenever I got out of sight of the house, I was with the gang. We would meet every evening about four blocks from where I lived. The boys would gather tin cans, boxes, and bells for instruments, and we would start a Cuban jam session. I fell in love with the sounds, the rhythms, the chants, the words—this was a wild crowd, and I loved every one of them.

A couple would get up and dance in the middle of the street. I watched carefully. My body would move in imitation of theirs. The rhythm would carry me away. I would yell encouragement, just as the others did. I was with them all the way.

Soon the boys began to invite me to the Cuban dances that were given every Friday, Saturday, and Sunday night in some dance hall or other. The price was fifty cents for girls, a dollar for boys. The only drinks that were served were soft drinks and beer. There was always a cop on hand to keep everyone under control, except when they were dancing—and the dances were wild, frenzied, and furious. I learned quickly and learned a lot in these dance halls.

I learned that boys thought me attractive, and, when they saw that I had good rhythm, they were willing to teach me their way of dancing as well as their way of talking. Soon I was one of the queens of the floor and could answer anyone who wanted to be smart, either in his language or my own.

I had a curfew to make every night, that of being home no later than seven in the evening. My few hours after school were lived fast and furious until curfew time. On Saturdays, I would get permission to stay out until ten, until I learned my aunt didn't get home until twelve at night because she had gotten another job.

When I came home from school during the week, I would do my homework and go out to join the gang—or I would join the gang and then come home to do homework. But on Saturdays, I would think of an excuse to stay out until ten at least. Sometimes I took the punishment of a whipping to stay out until the dance was over, which was around midnight. Of all the boys, Alex was the one everybody liked most. He was the one who was called on to do the fighting and lead the gang. He was lazy—didn't like school and stayed out all hours of the night. He was an only son and spoiled as the dickens, but very nice—at least I thought he was.

Alex was a soft-spoken, handsome, curly-haired brown-skin boy. I think I adored him more than I would ordinarily because every girl in the block wanted him. I was the one who had him, and I was perfectly satisfied with him.

Alex used to come around the corner, sloping his shoulders, head bent, smoking a cigarette. I waited with bated breath, hoping that he would smile at me when he saw me. Most of the time he would.

I kept getting a strange feeling about me that I secretly knew was one that longed for satisfaction, that had to do with physical contact. I didn't know how to go about this kind of thing. I was aware of the behavior between man and woman but deathly afraid of it. My aunt was afraid of it for me too. She knew I had come of age and had begun to notice the opposite sex, but she did not know how I was going about it. In her mind, as she often told me, I was a wild one. She did not realize how much fear she had put into me about men and their ways with women.

The first couple of days Alex and I were together, we talked about our lives at one stage of our youth or another. We would stand in the doorway of the candy store after it closed, or sit on a stoop somewhere in the block, gloating over each other, just holding hands or hugging. Most of the time we were silent or he would teach me a new phrase in Spanish. When I imitated his pronunciation, he would laugh until I got it right.

After I became Alex's girl he took me for a walk one night in Central Park, over by the lake. The moon was bright, the stars were out, and I was as usual my womanly self. The urge sprang up in me like a bat out of hell and so did fear. We sat on a bench watching the water from the lake glitter to and fro.

We watched the moon make love to the lake. The touch of his hand on mine brought a twang to the marrow in my bones. He knew I was young; so was he, but he knew, or at least I thought he knew, that I was not experienced at this sort of thing. What would I do if he started to go further than I expected him to? The thoughts of protection came to my mind. The thought of going ahead came to my mind.

The desire crept through me. Part of me was crying for the want of satisfaction. If he tries to kiss me, I will let him. Why doesn't he make the attempt? If I hold his hand tighter, maybe he will get the idea. I held tighter.

He took both of my hands; facing me, he looked me in the eye. "How old are you?" he asked.

"Fourteen."

"You haven't been around very much, have you?"

"What do you mean?"

"Well, I mean, well, you know what I mean."

"You don't like me because of that?"

"Sure. . . I like you, but. . . well. . ."

"Well what?"

"You know how the kids are in the block."

"You mean if the kids in the block are free with themselves, I must be too in order to be your girl?"

"No, but, well you know, everyone kids you when they know nothing is happening."

"Do they have to know? You mean all the kids get together and tell each other what they do with each other?"

"Well, you know how men are."

The feeling of my womanly wants suddenly disappeared. I no longer wanted him to kiss me or hold my hand or even talk. I started to pout. I sat in silence, looking into the water.

"I really don't care," he said, comforting me.

"Alex, what do you think of me?"

"What do you mean?"

"Do you think. I'm pretty?"

"Yes."

"Do you think I'm nice?"

"Yes."

"Would you rather be with someone else?"

"No, I don't think so."

"Who were you going with before?"

"Vickie."

"Do you still like her?"

"I like her, but I don't like her the way I like you."

"Does she still like you?"

"I don't know. She says she does."

"Why did you break up?"

"Oh, I don't know. We just broke up, that's all."

My femininity began to work. I got up, stretched. In order to make him think that I did not care, I decided to change the subject completely. I went back into my childish world. I walked to the nearest tree, sprang up to grab a hanging limb, and swung back and forth.

Alex looked at me with a smile on his face. In a showoff manner, I climbed like a chipmunk from one limb to another until I got to a resting place. Looking down from my heavenly perch, I laughed at him looking up at me. He stood in silence. I wondered what his thoughts were at this moment. Maybe he doesn't like me anymore. I will not let him know that I like him as much as I do. If he likes me, why doesn't he say so? Why must we play cat and mouse? I hate this kind of game, I decided.

"You better come down from there."

"Why?"

"It's pretty late."

'Tm going to stay up here forever. You won't ever be able to bring me to the park any more. Won't you be sorry?"

He laughed. "I'll go back to Vickie if you stay up there."

"I hate you," I screamed.

"Come on down and prove it."

In my pretense of fury I began to scramble out of the tree. As I reached the last hanging limb, I jumped, landing on my derriere. He laughingly picked me up.

In the fall I had bent one of my fingers backwards.

"It's broken," I said, holding it up to him.

"No, it isn't," he said.

"How do you know?" I panted.

"Well, it doesn't feel like it's broken."

"You don't even care if it is or not."

"I do care."

"Then why do you say it isn't?"

I wanted to hurt him. I wanted him to feel sorry for me. I wanted him to give me attention, attention and more attention. He looked at me, laughed, and said, "Oh, you poor baby," kissed me on my cheek and walked me home.

The next day I put a splint on my finger myself and bandaged it up to make it look worse than it was. My aunt looked at my hand and said, "Playing rough again, huh?" My playing rough was gradually becoming that of a woman and not a child.

One day in the new school, I learned how attractive I really was, or how much attention I caused. My teacher had kept me in the main building to talk to me one morning before my academic classes, which were in another building about two blocks away. This meant I had to walk to the Monroe building by myself.

As I walked along a brick wall that separated a group of apartments from the street, I noticed a group of boys huddling together. As I passed by them, the group moved quickly and enveloped me into their grouping.

"Where are you going?"

"I'm going to class."

One guy was big and muscular. "You wanna be my girl?" he asked.

I half smiled and tried to giggle my way clear. "I'm not interested in being anybody's girl," I said.

"Well, you're gonna be mine," I heard.

"If you wanna be my friend, okay," I said.

"Either you be my girl, or you'll be sorry," the boy said to me.

I became frightened. They looked tough, and it seemed this guy was the leader of them all. He was a bully, all right. They came close to me, and I felt a hand tightening on my arm. I wanted to scream for help, but this might frighten them and from revenge they might really get rough with me. By now I was really scared.

"If you don't like me," the boy said, "you'll learn to."

I stalled in hopes that something in my favor would happen. "Why aren't you boys in school?" I asked.

"Don't worry about us."

"I'm going to be late for my class."

"Well, why don't you answer our questions?"

"I told you, I don't wanna be anybody's girl."

"Well, ya better make up your mind, if you wanna go."

I tried to figure my way out of this horror, but nothing came to my mind. They had me pinned against the wall and were closing in. Then my prayers were answered. One of the teachers was coming. This made the boys slacken their hold on me and move off, leaving me to explain to the teacher why I was not in my class. I said nothing about the boys, though I wanted to. I suppose I was too scared. I made up some lie or other and was escorted to the building in peace.

After that, every time I had to go back and forth in the mornings or at noon, I tried to be surrounded by friends. As the months went by, I became more popular because of my acting and singing in assembly. But this worried me when it brought more attention from the boy gang. One boy would be sent to catch up with me and ask if I was ready to be the leader's girl. I would never answer. This caused a pulling of my hair or nasty words, or both. It seemed most of these boys, including the leader, lived in Brooklyn, so there was never any trouble on the subway.

One day as I came out of the main building to go home alone, one of the gang caught up to me. I talked to him as calmly as I could but was very nervous. When we reached the station, I went in the direction of the uptown subway. The boy put a tight grip on my arm. "You're going with me," he said.

"But I have to get home."

"I don't care about that, come on."

What is he going to do with me? Every thought under the sun came into my mind. How am I going to talk my way out of this? Besides, I only have a nickel; how am I going to get back? The boy pulled me along. He was determined to take me with him. On the subway to Brooklyn, he talked to me very calmly, but tough-like. Very sure of himself. I listened in agony.

He told me how I'd better give in to his leader because it would be too bad for me if I didn't. He told me his leader had never had his mind on girls before I came along and he had decided he wanted me.

"Why don't ya wanna be his girl?" I just looked at him. The toughness showed in his face. He looked as though he had had to fight for everything in life he wanted and no bones about it. I tried to bring out a little kindness, not for his sake, of course, but for mine. If I could weaken him, to make him give me a sincere smile instead of one of bitterness and revenge, I could encourage him to let me go back uptown. He wouldn't give.

His clothes were shabby, a little dirty, and he handled his books as though he didn't care about them. "You're not a bad-looking chick," he said. "You'd make somebody a good partner. I'd go for ya myself if he hadn't put his bid in first." He showed me he was afraid of this leader. He showed me, not in words, that getting me for his leader would put a feather in his cap. He showed me that he was just as scared as I was. We finally came to his stop. He got off and made me get off too. I walked down the stairs with his hand gripping my arm.

I wanted to pull away and run, but he would only get even with me in school. When we reached the street, he said, "You can go now." He walked away.

I stood there wondering what my next move should be. I walked back up the stairs, thinking up a nickel. I stood by the cashier's little room for what must have been fifteen minutes before I had enough nerve to tell the man I had gotten on the wrong train and didn't have another nickel. The man looked at me and without a smile pointed to the spoked gate and motioned for me to go through.

8

At home these days my aunt and I were rarely on speaking terms. I was becoming more and more afraid of her. When she came home, I cringed. If I was in the living room when she came in, I would go into the bedroom; if she came in there, I would go into the living room. She had no interest for me anymore. She used to tell me I would come to no good end.

"Don't talk to boys!"

"Clean this house."

"Why haven't you scrubbed the kitchen floor?"

"What are you reading for? Why can't you find something to do?"

"You've been in my things."

Being in her things was in her imagination. I knew how immaculate she was and how she hated having anything of hers disturbed. If an object of hers was moved half an inch on her dressing table, I would get a tongue lashing. I was afraid to dust for fear of touching anything. So I dusted around every object that was hers.

As the months went by, she began to leave me less and less money for school. I had to have a dime for subway fare, and at least fifty cents for lunch, that is, if I was to eat well. One morning I found a dime for carfare and a quarter. Then I found a dime and fifteen cents. I thought: she must be broke this week. I'll manage. Then I found a dime and a dime. Doesn't she care if I eat or not?

Half the time when I came home there was nothing but bread and milk. I began to worry, making up all kinds of excuses for her. She had been working hard in order to take care of me, but our relationship was growing thinner and thinner.

My clothes were getting shabby, so I had to think of ways to make them look decent. I would wash my blouse every night and iron it in the morning, until my aunt started complaining about the waste of electricity. When she hid the iron from me, I pressed my blouse on the steam pipe in the bathroom. This was done by pulling the blouse as hard as I could to and fro over the pipe. I had to get up half an hour earlier to do a good job.

Once I found a box hidden in the top of the closet. This box must have been there for a long time, though I could not remember ever seeing it. The clothes I found in it were completely out of style and hadn't been worn for years. My aunt must have forgotten about these things, I thought. She can't use this old blouse any more, and this old skirt I can make over for myself. I was too scared to ask her for these things and besides she probably wouldn't care, they were not serviceable to her. I went ahead and made me a nice little blouse and skirt.

About two weeks later, my aunt came home and found my newly made things. I got a mean whipping. When I told her the things had been rotting away up there in the closet, she said she knew it but they belonged to her and I had no business in her things. I suppose she was right.

One day I found only a dime to get to school. My aunt had left it faithfully on my table that morning. I went to school and sulked through lunch hour. This is all right, I thought, because when I get home there will be something to eat. But when I got home, the cupboard was bare. Anger swelled up inside my stomach and I slammed the door of the cupboard. I slammed the door of the smelly icebox that contained no ice, laid my head down on the kitchen table in my hands, and cried.

When my aunt came home that night, I didn't even look at her. She put her bundles down on a table, changed her clothes, and went out again. I made another search for food, found nothing.

Something must be wrong, I thought. My aunt can't deliberately do this to me. She knows I have no way of eating except through her. Maybe she's mad at me about something. What have I done? Everything wrong I had done she had already punished me for.

I was hurt more than I had ever been before. I could take the slaps, the beatings, the tongue lashings, as long as I knew what they were for. But this silence and food torture, I couldn't for the life of me forgive or understand.

In order to eat, I would visit friends and wait until dinner time, or I would sit around for hours in hopes that someone would get hungry and bring out some kind of food. Even a piece of bread was welcome. I couldn't let anyone know how starved I was, so at first I would refuse the offer of anything, but soon I lost my pride. In school, I would play up to the boys to get them to take me to lunch.

My teacher, who was a very good friend, noticed that I was not very happy or that something was wrong. She would try to get me to talk, but I remained silent. Sometimes my teacher would keep me after school to try and get information about my home life. I wanted badly to tell her about my troubles, but I couldn't. Sometimes she would treat me to lunch or take me for an ice cream sundae. It gave me great joy to know that someone cared.

When my teacher or someone made me laugh, you could hear it for miles, because it burst from my body and thundered out. It came like a hail of rain breaking its way from the sky. I laughed with all of me, thankful for the excuse. When I cried, I cried alone. I began to pity myself and build a hate inside of me that was to bring me more pain as I grew older.

I began to think of myself as a tortured child. I began to think that I really was a good-for-nothing. I leaned more and more to myself.

One day I saw a sign outside a store announcing the need of a school worker. Without a second thought, I went in and applied for the job. It was a job of putting writing paper and envelopes in a box.

I said I could work from the time I got out of school until seven. I got the job and it paid me about seven dollars a week. This was fine; now I didn't have to depend on my aunt to give me school money. I was independent of her. That is, until she inquired.

When she learned I was earning seven whole dollars a week, she said this was fine, but seven dollars was too much money for a young girl to have, so she took my weekly pay and continued to give me enough money to get to school, including a quarter for lunch.

This job didn't last very long, because instead of coming right home from school, I didn't get home until nine. One night after my little job, I came home and found the whole apartment ransacked. Someone had broken in and searched the place. I was so frightened I didn't know what to do. I saw the bedroom window was broken.

What will my aunt say when she comes home? All her things scattered all over—she'll give me a whipping because I wasn't home. Maybe I can cover everything up, put everything back in its place, nice and neat. She won't even know. In nervousness I succeeded in replacing everything. Then I went to bed and tried to sleep. I was too scared to go to sleep. I finally got up and decided to wait in a chair by the door, with a stick in my hand to protect myself in case the burglar decided to return. When my aunt came in, she was surprised to see me sitting there wide-eyed, looking at her.

"What are you doing up with that stick?" I told her what I had found when I came in. She searched the house to see if anything was missing. Nothing was.

After a while, it seemed that I had done too good a job replacing things, because she turned to me and said, "You're lying. No one came into this house. You went through my things looking for money. You got scared that I might notice, broke the window, and made up that lie about a burglary." I was more surprised to hear her story than she was to hear mine. How could she think I would do a thing like that? What kind of a child did she think I was? She really doesn't like me. She hates me.

"You're nothing but a no-good. I knew I shouldn't have brought you up here. I should have left you down South to pick cotton like the rest of them, for the rest of your life."

How can I tell her I didn't do it?

"I'm tired of having to look out for you. You don't know how much agony you've caused me, having to feed you and clothe you. . . ."

Now I knew. She had grown tired of having such a great responsibility. Never having been married, never having had any children of her own, she no longer cared if I lived or died.

She almost had her wish, because a few days later, as I walked to the subway alone in hopes of catching up with my girlfriends who usually waited for me, I was confronted by the gang again. This time they all followed me, nagging and yelling. I ran down the stairs to the train. I heard it coming in the distance. As I looked down the platform, I saw some of my friends. I caught their eyes as they caught mine and we all began to run towards each other in order to get into the same car.

Just as I reached them, the train came blasting into the station. We were almost at the beginning of the platform, so the train was still going full speed. I felt myself being pushed hard. Before I could realize it, my girlfriend grabbed my clothing and yanked.

The boys ran down the platform, laughing among themselves as my friends calmed me and themselves at the thought that I had almost been killed. Those boys must have really had it in for me.

Eartha Kitt, aged sixteen,
Metropolitan High School,
New York

School group, some months la

While touring in Mexico

Early days with
Katherine Dunham

A scene from Orson Welle's
Paris production of Faust

On her trip to Turkey

1950

Paris, 1949

Turkey, 1950

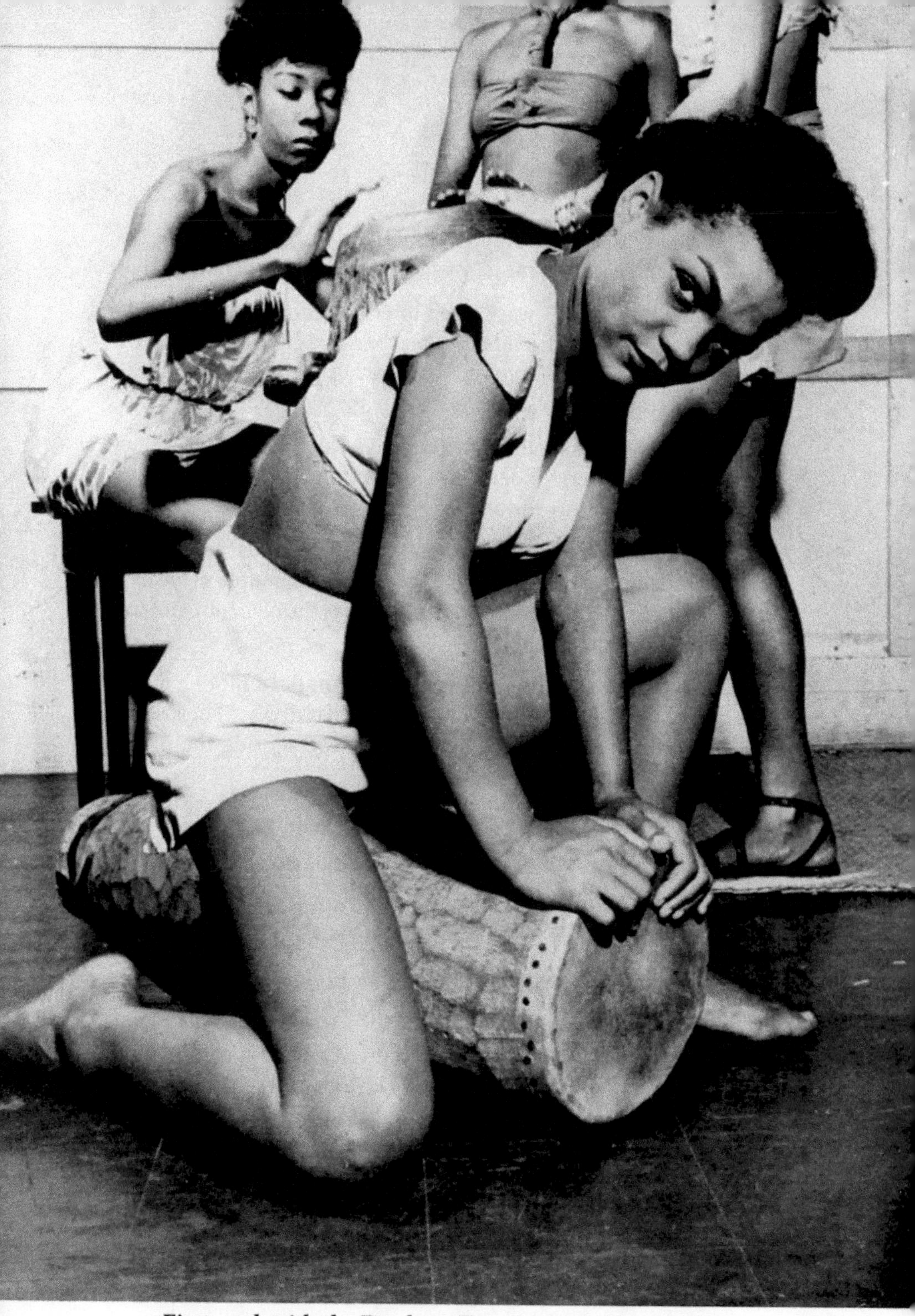

First week with the Dunham Troupe, September 1946

We didn't say much about it on the way home. All the kids got off at my stop and escorted me to my door to see that I got home safely.

The next morning I was scared to go to school but went under the protection of my friends. My teacher said nothing to me, but she obviously knew about it. My teacher and my friends got together, I learned later, and went to the principal about it.

After a few weeks, none of these boys were seen at the school. They were all drafted suddenly into the Army. My life at school was peaceful again, but my life at home got worse.

I obtained a job as a salesgirl in a shoe store not far from where I lived. I made about ten dollars a week. After a couple of weeks, I bought myself a new dress and a pair of shoes the owner of the store let me have for half price.

I thought this would cause comment from my aunt one way or the other, and it did. "Where did you get that dress?" she asked. I told her I had been working. "Why didn't you bring the money home before you went off and spent it?"

"I wanted to work to buy nice things for school," I said.

"Don't you know it costs money to take care of you?"

"I thought it would be all right to buy something I needed and to show you I was not throwing the money away."

"If you want to work, bring the money home to help me pay the rent and buy food."

No matter what I did, it turned out to be wrong, so I began to find excuses to stay out later at night. During the week I came home at night around nine because I had to get up early to go to school. But came the weekend, I would stay at a Cuban dance until it was over. I started coming home around one on Fridays and Saturdays.

My aunt said nothing for a long time. Then one night when I came home after one of the dances, she met me at the door and said,

"Give me my key." I gave her the key. "Get out of this house and don't come back. You're a tramp, a no-good. You stay out all hours of the night. Nobody knows where you are. One day you'll turn up pregnant, and then who'll have to take care of you—me. I don't want anything like that in my house. Go on back in the street where you belong."

Little did my aunt know that I was too shy of boys even to let one kiss me. I never had the desire to smoke or drink. When I stayed out late, I wanted to maintain my self-respect by being what I called "a good girl." My chief reason for late hours was that I thought she didn't care what I did anyway.

I walked to the subway, paid a nickel, and made the train my hotel for the night. When it was day, I went to a friend's house and stayed there all day. When the evening came, I went to a movie and saw a picture three or four times. When night came again, I slept on the roof. For the first time, I knew what a bum must feel like.

I was too proud to tell any of my friends my troubles. I mingled with the kids of the neighborhood, laughing and joking as though my life was well in hand. The following night I managed to get my girlfriend to invite me to spend the night with her.

I didn't go to school for a couple of days. I couldn't because my clothes were too dirty, and I couldn't figure out how to go home for clean ones.

After sleeping wherever I could, in doorways, on roofs, and at friends' homes for a while, I decided the best thing for me to do was to get a job. A friend of mine took me to a factory and got me employed, with a fake birth certificate, as a seamstress. It was a factory of about thirty employees where Army clothes were sewed and mended.

I quit school completely. I was myself again after a few days' work and a few good meals. I began to laugh all the time, tell jokes, and sing at my machine. I was becoming popular at the factory because I sang all the time—Cuban songs, Negro spirituals, all kinds of songs. Everyone in the factory waited for me to start singing.

I had gotten a room in the Bronx with a Cuban family who liked me very much. The mother of the house didn't speak English very well, so I had to learn Cuban better to talk with her. This was fun, because I felt I was getting something accomplished.

One night as I sat at my machine in a very happy spirit (I worked from five until twelve), the floor manager came to me and said I was wanted in the main office. Those who heard her turned to look in curiosity.

"What do they want to see me for?" I asked.

"I don't know," the woman answered.

I pulled myself together and marched to the office. They must have found out about my birth certificate. As I walked into the main office, a man looked at me, fiddling with some papers in his hands.

"Your name Eartha Kitt?"

"Yes, sir."

"Your aunt claims you've run away from home. Why?"

"Why what, sir?"

"Why did you run away?"

I couldn't tell him that I had not run away, that my aunt had put me out.

"Don't you like your aunt?"

"Yes, sir."

"What does the trouble seem to be?" I remained silent. "She is very worried about you." How could she be worried about me if she was the one who told me to leave? I thought. "You know children who run away from home are put into a special home for kids if they persist in this kind of action."

"Yes, sir."

"Do you want to talk to us about it?"

"No, sir."

They must know how old I am to talk like that. They can't put you away unless you're under eighteen, and my false birth certificate says I'm eighteen. I had just turned fifteen in January, and this was the end of January.

"I'll give you until midnight tonight to get home."

I walked back to my machine and continued my work, thinking of how I was going to greet my aunt, or how she was going to greet me. She must be sorry about what happened. Now maybe we can be friends.

The snow was thick on the New York streets as I marched meekly to my aunt's house, knocked on the door, expecting a smiling warm face to greet me, saying she was sorry, in order for me to say I was sorry and let's forgive and forget and live happily ever after.

"Oh, it's you," she said. No smile, no greeting, no kind word. A cold back was turned to me, as she went back to bed.

I walked in. If she would only give me a smile. Why did she make me come back? She must have felt guilty for putting me out. If anything really happened to me, she would be responsible for it. But if I leave home on my own, she can blame anything that happens on me.

I went into the bathroom, washed my hair, took a bath, got clean clothes, put on my clothes and coat, walked out. Into the snow and slush, with wet hair and damp body. A few days later, I took very ill. My body was very weak.

I had found a room closer to where I was working, with a man and his wife. I didn't want to tell them I was ill because this would make them uncomfortable. I walked around the house in agony, trying to stay on my feet. I had to lie down every few minutes. I stayed home, didn't go to work, and was very silent. I resorted to locking myself in my room, only coming out when they had left the house in order to get myself some soup or something to keep me alive.

I was like this for about two weeks, so I lost my job. I went back to school and explained to my teacher that I was ill and that I had not been living with my aunt. She told me I had a lot of grades to make up, so I'd better get busy. I had a little money left from my factory job to pay my carfare for a while, but I had to get another job if I wanted to keep going. This began to worry me, because it was difficult to hold a job and do my schoolwork too.

Then one day, who should walk into my classroom but my aunt. She told my teacher I had run away, or something to this effect, and that she wanted me home. My teacher talked to me and made me realize that my place was with my aunt.

My aunt and I were at peace with one another for a whole month. She came home with a smile, had food in the house to eat, gave me money for school, and everything was fine. But as the days grew warmer, my aunt became filled with the idea that I was too big for her to be taking care of. I should have a job to take care of myself. She began to complain about me being home all the time. Why was I reading again? Scrub the floors, make up the beds, practice the piano—she was becoming more nervous of me.

My aunt's boyfriend would come in once in a while on leave from the Army. I was glad when he was around, because he liked me. Once in a while he would give me a whole dollar for running an errand or fifty cents just for being me.

He would talk to me for hours and laugh to see how well I knew how to speak Spanish. He and I would converse in Spanish for a long time while my aunt sat and listened, not being able to understand. He would tell me Cuban jokes to make me laugh. I had to repeat them to him to be sure I could remember them. This would go on, on Saturdays and Sundays.

He used to take up for me too. When he was home, I knew I was noticed. "You're not treating that child right," he would say to my aunt.

"It's none of your business how I treat her."

"I know. That's why I don't interfere any more than I do, but you have no gentleness with her. She wants to be loved, like any child does."

"What makes you think I don't?"

I noticed the word love never entered my aunt's mouth. She always avoided that one word. I listened closely to these discussions between them, but there was never a satisfactory conclusion to any of them. It was nice of him to take up for me, but there was really no use, except he did put hope in my heart.

One night he saved my life, or at least it looked that way. I had gotten my aunt angry about something, I don't remember what, though I think it had something to do with my piano lessons.

Anyway, she got mad. As I huddled in a corner of the bedroom on a stool, she came down on me with all her might with the ironing cord. I covered my head and face, and held tight with every muscle in order not to cry. I wouldn't cry, I refused to cry.

As she stopped for a minute, I raised my head and looked her straight in the eye. This angered her more. She had brought no tears. She came down again and again. "You miserable little wretch. All I do is work and slave for you. You're no good, you hear me, no good."

Just as she was about to walk away, I raised my head again, to show her I was stronger than the ironing cord and all her muscles. Her face turned red from madness. She pulled the stool from under me. I went to the floor on my knees. She raised the stool high above her head and was about to come down on me when her boyfriend walked into the room, took the stool out of her hand, and walked out of the house, slamming the door behind him.

9

I left home again. I went back with the Cuban family in the Bronx, got another job that was in Brooklyn. This job lasted for a couple of months as I found I could make quite a bit of money working overtime. My duty was to walk up and down a machine that was at least a mile long, looking for empty bobbins. If a bobbin was empty, I had to tell the foreman to have it threaded again.

The machine, along with four others like it, made Swiss-like embroidery and emblems for soldiers' uniforms. I worked from nine in the morning until six or seven in the evening. My pay was sixty-some dollars a week. The people in this factory were young and very interested in me. They too learned I could sing, so again I went about my work with a song, walking up and down with a light in my hand, on the hunt for empty bobbins. In our spare time, we would all sit around and talk about ourselves, what we did, had done, and our intentions for the future.

My intention for the future was to become a person of the theater. I told them how my teacher had encouraged me to go into the theater, and how she had prepared me for an audition for *Carmen Jones*. I was given carfare by her, told to put on my best dress, and take the classical music that I had learned. She gave me a pass for the theater that *Carmen Jones* was playing at. I told them how scared I was sitting up in a balcony all by myself to see the show. It was very exciting. I wondered at the dancing, I marveled at the singing and the scenery.

When the play was over, I had to go backstage and ask for a Mister So-and-so. He was to take care of me after that. Backstage was not easy to find. I walked into more stone walls and through more doors that led nowhere than ever before. When I finally found the door that led to the stage, I didn't know what to do after I got there. There was a man sitting at a piano. There was a man standing onstage, holding a book. A man and a woman were fussing in the empty seats of the theater.

I stood on the side, waiting for someone to notice me. The someone who did was gentle and calm. He took my music, gave it to the pianist, announced to the man in the empty seats that if he was ready to start the auditions, so were we.

The piano started to play. I wrung my hands, got choked, swallowed, thought of the things I'd rather have been doing, and prayed.

When the piano got to the part where the singer was supposed to sing, I sang, but nothing came out that was audible. We started again. The faces were cold and calm. The theater was cold and quiet. The chairs were empty and ugly. Why didn't they turn on some lights? No one could see a thing.

"Because you come to me. . ." My song finally got started and was coming out of me like a whistle through a bamboo stick. Then it got stronger almost at the end. I was really in good voice as I sang the last four measures: "Because you come to me with naught save love."

As I was bowed and thanked out of the stage door, a member of the cast said to me, "Why didn't you sing the whole song as you did the last few bars?" I could not give him an answer. I just smiled and was thankful that I was not accepted.

Another time my teacher sent me to the theater to see Jose Ferrer in *Cyrano de Bergerac*. I never got over his long nose. I adored him. I loved the way he talked his love lines. I loved the way he moved around the stage. I loved the love he loved and cried the cries he cried. I was brokenhearted at the end, when he was brokenhearted. I left the theater in a daze, walking to Fifth Avenue from Seventh to catch a bus. My heart laughed and cried all at the same time.

I looked out of my eyes with a new light. I saw the world in a different color. Everything was rosy, lavender gray, and alive. The people were alive, the buildings swayed to and fro. The skies moved about but I stood still in a daze of warmth. If I could do this, do the same thing he did. If I could give the feeling of happiness to people, or to anyone for that matter, that he gave to me. If I only knew how. If only I had the gumption, the chance.

The wonderment of this kind of world began to haunt me. A world of giving and taking. A world of independence and fascination. I could do it, I kept telling myself. I could do that.

I hated the idea of going back to that factory. I hated the idea of having a routine life, of having to get up at seven A.M. to get to school, of having knowledge from books crowded into my head. I wanted to rebel. I wanted to change the world to be the way I wanted it. I wanted a law forbidding people to work longer than four hours a day at the most. People should be independent of restrictions. Restrictions of society, of laws. People should not be made to do things they did not like. I began to rebel.

I felt the important thing for people was to eat when they were hungry, not because it was breakfast time, lunchtime, dinnertime or suppertime. One should work when he needed to work to earn enough to feed and clothe a family properly, to have a home when he wanted to have it. To love because he loved, to hate because he hated, not because someone told him to, when, where, and how.

I hated the idea of having to be in a certain place at a certain time. I should go when I wanted. No one should be obligated to anyone.

The thoughts about how I wanted the world to be were muddled in my mind. I knew these things could never come about, but this did not keep me from dreaming them. I knew what I wanted, even if it was hard for me to put it into words.

At the age of fifteen, began to feel as though I were growing up, not physically, because this I was already well aware of, but inside. I wanted more than anything in the world to know how to think, to be able to make decisions for myself. I wanted a bright mind, one that knew where it was going and why. was not looking for anything definite, but I wanted to see beyond yesterday, to have a feeling for tomorrow.

I didn't want the world on a string, or to sit on a rainbow. All I wanted was a spark. A spark to give me hope. Since I knew I could not get that spark from my aunt or from anyone I knew at the moment, I set out to find it away from home. I became an adventuress. That is to say, I no longer felt afraid of anything, I no longer felt afraid of being hurt by anything, except people. I began to grow immune to hunger, to physical hurts.

I wanted to think of myself as a human being, not a person belonging to any one nationality or to a people but to the whole wide world. I didn't want to be conscious of the fact that my skin was black or brown or white or gray, or that my eyes were blue or brown. I wanted to be me, to have a place in the world to call my own. When I wanted to share it, I would share it. If I wanted it alone, I would be alone.

What I wanted was confused in my mind. I had to learn how to clarify it. To put it into words, to simplify it, to make someone else understand how I felt inside.

My eyes looked with suspicion and questions at the rest of the world. Why was I born, why was I living? To be what I wanted to be, to think as I wanted to think, to act as I wanted to act, to speak as I wanted to speak—or to do what the world wanted?

I wanted to know how to discipline myself to my own restrictions, to my own thoughts, not to anyone else's. To discipline myself to know what was right and what was wrong, and act accordingly. I wanted to do what I liked, and what I did not like I wanted to leave alone. I wanted a world of my own. To let in those I loved and to keep out those I did not care for.

What I did not know was that I was becoming suspicious of everyone that tried to break into my world. I began to analyze people, but I forgot to analyze myself. This was not important. People should accept me as I was or not at all. The only thing that mattered to me was how people affected me, not how I affected them. Years later, I learned that the world was a form of give and take, not just take. I also learned that I should give freely of myself, without expectations.

That summer I joined the farmerettes. To get away from New York, away from my aunt, to think things out. Before I went I told everyone in the factory that I was going to become a dancer, that I was going to have an audition for a dance troupe. Everyone in the factory wished me luck and hoped for the best for me. Everyone was amazed. I said I was sure I would get the job because I could dance very well. The truth of the matter was I knew nothing whatsoever about dancing, except what I had learned in the Cuban dance halls. When I said good-by to the factory, I had no idea what I was going to do, but I went and applied for a farmerette's job, which meant being in a camp of about a thousand girls to help out on the farms in upstate Connecticut.

The obligation was to earn not less than ten dollars a week for room and board, picking onions out of the ground, or cherries from the trees, or currants from bushes, or hoeing the land.

I soon was in demand because I was a good worker. I won a contest picking currants at five cents a quart. My earnings ran up to fifty and sixty dollars a week, which I spent on goodies, or I would take a bus on Saturday to New York.

I stayed at this camp all summer. When I returned to New York in September, I went back to live with the Cuban family. After a few days, a girlfriend and I decided to take in a downtown movie. I had enough money for both of us. The movie house was very crowded and I became nervous from being among so many people. I wanted to leave. There was only standing room.

"If you don't want to leave, I'm going to leave you."

"Let's stay and see the stage show. It's coming on now," she said.

I managed to stand very nervously and uncomfortably among the people who insisted on doing the same. When the stage show came on, I was glad because this was what I had wanted to see. Carmen Miranda twitched around the stage and went *sheeboom, sheeboom.* I twitched around in my place and wondered what there was about her that all these people would stand up to see. I soon found out. All I could think of as I left the theater was her twitching and *sheeboom, sheeboom.*

As we stood outside of the theater on Broadway, wondering what to do, whether we should spend a dime for candy, we noticed a girl pacing up and down, looking at the buildings as though she was looking for something. She reminded me of me, when I first came up North. She saw us looking at her, and came over and asked, "Can you tell me where Max Factor's make-up shop is?"

I asked her if she had the address. She did, so we took her there. Not only that, we went in to see what she was buying and why. I knew all about make-up, because this had been part of our drama work in school, but why was she buying all this theatrical make-up?

As our conversation went on, I learned she was a Katherine Dunham dancer and that the make-up was for Miss Dunham.

"I'd love to meet Miss Dunham," I said.

"Well, why don't you come down to the school with me and I'll introduce you? As a matter of fact, she is looking for dancers. Can you dance?"

"Oh, yes, I can dance very well," I lied.

"She is having auditions now. Come and go with me."

When we arrived at the school, there was a group dancing, and more dancers were prancing up and down the studio. We stood in the door and watched for a while. Then I got cold feet.

"Go on," my girlfriend said.

"No, she won't like me."

"How do you know?"

"Well, you know I can't dance like that."

"Those kids don't look so hot either," my friend said. "Besides, you are always dancing around the house, doing acrobatic things and whatnot. Just do some of the things you do at the house."

"Nooooo."

"I dare you."

"I don't have any dancing clothes."

A tall woman came up to us and asked us if we were going to audition.

"I'm not, she is," my friend said.

"The dressing room is upstairs," the woman said.

"Go on upstairs. Maybe someone will give you something to wear. If not, audition in what you have on."

When I got upstairs, an older girl did give me a garment to wear. She had obviously been around the business for a long time. I changed my clothes and began to practice what I was going to do on the dance floor.

"I really don't know how to do anything," I kept saying, doing a split on the floor, doing a head stand, kicking my feet up in the air, and contorting my body into various positions. "What should I do?" I kept saying.

"Oh, just go down and follow the leader," the girl said. Finally I was called on to join the rest who either would prove themselves dancers or be told to go back where they came from. The group stood in a corner of the room and watched the leader. Whatever he did, we were to imitate. I watched every arm, foot, head, and body movement until I thought I had it.

I went down the floor, imitating what I had seen as closely as I could, getting into everyone's way. I moved my pelvis freely and worked my feet furiously. I was terribly disappointed when any part of me would not work right. I wanted to give up but why not continue? I wiggled and twitched, bounced, and exhausted myself. Then it was over.

I sat on a chair against the wall of the room, where my girlfriend sat waiting. The tall woman came over finally and asked, "Can you be here Monday morning at ten?"

"Well, I guess so," I answered in surprise. "Why?"

"You've won a scholarship."

PART TWO

1

MY DAY at the Katherine Dunham school began at ten in the morning, with a ballet class, a thing I had had no conception of. The dancing I liked most of all was the Dunham technique. It started a half hour after the ballet and went on for about one and a half hours. Before the dancing, we would all start at the bar with warmups. This was not very strenuous for me, for I was always active and kept my body limbered up. I could do just about anything with myself, but when it came to using real strength, I found my thighs were rather weak. I worked hard the first few weeks, then found myself getting lazy, as I am naturally lazy except when I really have to prove myself. With something to compete with, I have a hard time holding in. Being alone has taught me a lot. You can't just be good; you have to be better than good.

After a few days I became acquainted with most of the kids in the school. The ten dollars a week we received from our scholarships was not enough to let us be extravagant in any way, barely comfortable, but we were grateful to get it. We could not take any outside jobs because our hours were too long. I thought nothing of this, having extra money I mean, until the woman from whom I rented a room started on me about paying the rent. I tried to figure out a way to pay her at least five dollars a week and have five for carfare, but I soon ran into trouble because five dollars was not enough for transportation and food too. I kept saying, "I'll pay you."

The little money I had saved up before I came into the school, I loaned out to some of the kids. This was a mistake because the borrowing never ceased. Even some of the five dollars I kept for the subway and lunch was soaked up in loans.

I didn't know exactly why I was so generous, but I had always been this way. Maybe it was because I wanted to be liked and I didn't care what price I had to pay for attention. Maybe it was because I wanted them to be obligated to me. Anyway, I knew what I was doing and had no intention of stopping it. The one person who befriended me, defended me, and loved me regardless, was Roxie Foster. She laughed about my quirks, talked to me about them, and called me her friend.

About a month after I joined the school, Miss Dunham came back from a tour in California. We all knew she was coming to the school to pick some of us for a new show that was being prepared for Broadway. When the day arrived, she came into the studio with her secretary and other members of her entourage and sat quietly while the audition went on.

"Will I be chosen?" My head said yes, but how could I be sure? If you have doubts and you are chosen, then you'll be surprised. Don't gamble on it. Remember you don't want to be hurt. Disappointments always hurt. You're really not a very good dancer, but she might think you have possibilities.

She obviously did, because I was chosen. The next day, she started work on the choreography for the new show. It was a dance of the South Sea Islands. All the girls were to come on stage in a Polynesian movement, as though coming from the jungle. We were to be spotted by a sailor, who would go into his own dance to try to attract one of the girls. This little episode caused a little disturbance, for Miss Dunham had chosen a person for this who we thought was good, but when we went into rehearsals at the theater he was replaced. For a while there was quite a bit of fussing about our routine, because of various people with various ideas as to how we should come on stage and perform. Miss Dunham herself had returned to California, and we had no one to look out for us except our teacher, who was in charge while Miss Dunham was away. There were times when we were helpless little souls, a herd of sheep without our shepherd.

The show contained many known entertainers—Ethel Waters, Willie Bryant, and many others, including Josh White—Josh White, a man I shall never forget. I remember the first day I saw him. He walked into the rehearsal studio with his guitar, went to the piano, stuck a cigarette in the side of his mouth, and plucked.

The sound of his music box twanged my womanliness. It edged my senses and wined my bittered blood. I watched his hands, as they told of love and hatred, of sensuous love and faithless women. His mouth moved as though he was making love to the words he spoke, but they did not make love to him. His eyes dimmed with "Come hither, so that I may suck you in. There's no woman I cannot have and any woman can have me."

"Who's that?" I asked Roxie.

"Don't you know who that is? That's Josh White."

I said nothing, still not knowing who Josh White was. I went nearer, so that I could sense him better and to make him sense me. When his eyes met mine, our senses touched. He finished his song to me. When the rehearsal was over, we went our different ways, to meet again the next day.

One night, I should say morning, after rehearsal, he offered to take Roxie and me home, as I was living with her then. Roxie lived on Convent Avenue with her mother. She shared her room with me. We pooled our money to make ends meet and we got along very well. I had explained to Roxie that the woman I roomed with wanted more money for rent than I could afford to pay. So Roxie told me I could stay with her for a while. It was very comfortable there, so I stayed on, probably longer than she or her mother anticipated.

The show in which we did our South Seas number, *Blue Holiday*, lasted only five days in New York, which put us right back where we started, but the rehearsal money was a bit more than we were accustomed to getting, so we were a little better off than before. At least we were eating better. I never got to see much of the show because we were always busy changing costumes or something.

Josh asked me to go out to dinner with him one night. My first time in a real night club was exciting. I meekly trailed behind Josh as he was greeted by everyone. The owners, the musicians, the waiters, the clients—everyone seemingly liked him. I was proud to be with him.

He sat me at a table with some friends of his and told one of the waiters to pay special attention to me. This gave me a feeling of importance. No one had ever treated me so royally. Since I did not drink, I asked the waiter for something to eat, a steak—the first one I remember ever eating.

The drums began to roll, the lights went down, everyone got quiet, and the show started. Imogene Coca came out in a dim light. She stood in front of a mike. The people began to smile, much to my surprise, but I learned a few minutes later that they laughed because she was a comedienne. Knowing this, the people began to laugh in expectation. She was the funniest woman I had ever seen and the funniest I have seen until this day, besides Bea Lillie. Fact is, I don't remember Josh's act that night but Imogene Coca stuck in my mind.

Miss Dunham had returned to New York a day or so before *Blue Holiday* closed. Again she selected new members for her company. Again I was one chosen. We went back to school, which had moved from Fifty-ninth Street to Forty-third Street. Our hours were about the same, from eleven to eleven. Classes during the day and rehearsals at night. This time it was a show called *Carib Song*. I didn't know much about it, but I knew Dunham was going to act.

During these months of rehearsals and training, with our ten dollars a week from Miss Dunham, we lived on hot dogs and cokes. There were many days when some of us sneaked back into the school at night to sleep because we had no place to stay. Miss Dunham, of course, did not know this. We would spread out the Haitian straw mats on the studio floor, cover ourselves with what clothing we had, and be up and out before anyone came in to open the school in the morning.

We would pool our dimes for a coffee breakfast and spend the remaining dimes in a movie until time for class. When Miss Dunham taught on Sunday afternoons for the backers' benefit, we all worked hard to please her. This we enjoyed more than anything. Her choreography was unquestionable. Each of us longed for her to choreograph a dance featuring us.

"Go sit by the body that's dead and gone," we sang. We lifted a huge basket, bringing it on the stage, waving our hands to the men meeting us on the stage. "Is she watching me? Does she think I am good? I didn't do that movement very well, but wait until I do the next one."

Not having enough money to give ourselves good rehearsal clothes, most of us did manage to have clean ones, in envy of the beautiful clothes Miss Dunham always had. Hand-knitted tights, with a hand-knitted sweater to match, or a skirt and blouse effect with long tights underneath. She always looked like the essence of success to me. Her husband, Mr. John Pratt, was always there, cheering her on, seeing that she dressed properly, making new clothes for her, or maybe just for moral support.

Miss Dunham, being tall with erect stature, reminded me very much of my aunt, but there was no other resemblance. When she walked into the room, no matter what I was doing, I would stop to look at her, in hopes that she would say, "Hello, Kitty"—everyone called me Kitty. Sometimes she did, sometimes she didn't, but I always hoped she would stop and joke with us. Each of us would be in his glory to be able to laugh at something she did or said. Every time she reprimanded a member of the class for not doing good work, the others were relieved not to be the one, with a false feeling of being her favorite.

When you come right down to it, we were all pretty dependent on our leader. We would talk about her unmercifully—anything to downgrade her in our own eyes because she held a power over us that we could not understand and that we resented. At the same time, we idolized her, for the courage and strength to accomplish what she had, for her leadership and protection. We did feel protected with her. We were afraid to leave and afraid to stay. Once in a while Miss Dunham would give us a lecture on not getting discouraged. She said that the outside world was cruel and hard, that we didn't know how well off we were to be getting this training and experience. We would find many faults with this kind of talk. She was holding us back—once we decided to leave the company we would prove ourselves in no time, we thought. At times I thought Miss Dunham was unfair, but I knew too that she had to fight hard in order to survive. I wondered sometimes why she never gave us a better chance of showing off our talents. It wasn't until years later that I learned for myself just how true most of her words were about the outside world being difficult and about that long narrow rocky path to success and what the word, success, really meant.

After six months or so of rehearsals, we did *Carib Song*, with Avon Long as Dunham's leading man. It was a love story with music. Dunham sang, danced, and acted. I still remember a song, "Sleep baby, don't cry," sung by Harriet Jackson, who made my heart sick when she sang behind a jungle screen as Dunham danced. The show lasted for a couple of months on Broadway, after trying out in New Haven, and once more we went back to school, this time to prepare for *Bal Nègre*, another revue.

During this period, I moved in with Nickie and another friend I got along very well with. The next year or so consisted of living again on ten dollars a week and eating wherever we could. If someone invited us to a party, we accepted gladly. Our only aim was food. To get a meal we accepted dates with boys we didn't care for. I never could understand why men would offer you a drink quicker than food.

One day I was left at the house alone because it was Sunday. I don't know where the others went. It was what we called a private house, at One Hundred and Forty-fifth Street and St. Nicholas Avenue. A friend of ours who was a party-giver lived next door in the back apartment. He was out, but before he left he told me to say he'd be back at such and such an hour if anyone called.

Around four in the afternoon, someone knocked on my door. "Who is it?" I asked.

A familiar voice said, "A friend of Rick's next door."

I opened the door. "Rick isn't home," I answered.

"I know Rick isn't home." The handsome boy sneered. "It's you I want."

When I tried to close the door, I found a foot holding it open. He walked in, looking around to see if anyone was with me. I tried to act as though I could handle myself, but fear struck me. I had seen him around the neighborhood.

He sat in a chair as I fiddled with a comb and brush on the dresser. I pretended to fix my hair in preparation for going out. I could see him in the mirror. He slouched, making himself comfortable as he glared at me with desirous eyes. I must get out of this somehow. I tried to pretend everything was normal and proper.

He took hold of my arm, pulling me to him. "You gonna be a good girl?"

"What do you mean, a good girl?" I asked, pulling away.

"Don't gimme that. You know what I mean." I laughed weakly, walking around the room. The door was so near and yet so far. How can I get out? I went back to combing my hair. He got up, stood in back of me, and felt the texture of my loosely combed locks. "Nice hair," he said. "Pretty—"

"Thank you," I answered, afraid to move.

When I tried to move, he had me pinned to the dressing table with his body. He put one arm around my body and said, "Don't scream or do anything funny. I'm here for one thing, so you better be nice." At this point I felt something pressing my side. "Come over to the bed."

When I turned I saw a knife long enough to kill a mule. With my knees weakened, my mind began to work. He led me to the bed. "Listen," I said in a low voice, "you don't have to try to take anything from me. I know you—you know me. Why do we have to fight each other?"

"What do you mean?" I moved to look out the window. "Don't go near the window. My boys are all waiting for me on the stoop, so you're trapped."

"Oh, I'm not going to try anything—" There were boys on the stoop, mingling, talking, standing around with nothing to do. They might be with him—couldn't tell—maybe he's bluffing.

He came and pulled down the shade. "Get back over to the bed."

"Why do you want to act like this?" I asked. "When you're a man and I am a woman, why don't we act like it?"

"What do you mean?"

"Well, you're not a bad-looking guy and you want me, right?"

"Go on."

"It would be much simpler for us to have some pleasure out of this—" He gave me a suspicious look. "How can you expect a girl with a knife in her ribs to give freely so that you could enjoy her?"

By this time I was sitting on the bed comfortably, thinking of another scheme in case this one did not work.

"You mean you wouldn't mind?"

"Why should I? I'd rather go through with this freely than be forced. That's no fun."

"You're all right, you know that? Not only that, you're smart." He began to laugh. "I didn't know it would be this easy. Okay, let's get started."

"Wait a minute now, since we agree, don't you think I should protect myself? Suppose I get messed up or something—you wouldn't want that, would you?"

"Oh, I didn't think about that."

"Well, I've got something upstairs in the bathroom. I'll be back in a minute." He looked at me with that look of control, putting his hand on the door as I moved toward it. "I can't possibly get out. Your boys would stop me, wouldn't they?"

"Okay, but don't be long."

I went out into the hallway. The boys were still standing laughing it up on the stoop. I wondered if they were really with him. I ran upstairs so that he could hear my footsteps going up. I stood at the top for about a minute or so, to see if he would look outside or something. He did not. Then step by step I sneaked down the long flight without a sound. I listened at the door for a sign of life. Then I moved slowly to the street door. If the boys tried to stop me I would scream, I thought, and maybe someone would hear me.

I walked out as though everything was orderly and proper, went through the group and down the stairs to the sidewalk. No one noticed particularly. The moment I hit the pavement I took out like lightning for the subway. I would lose myself this way; he wouldn't be able to find me. I wound up at a friend's house on One Hundred and Fifty-third Street and stayed there for the rest of the night.

After this I moved in with two girl friends on Forty-fifth Street. There were two rooms. In one Madeline stayed, in the other Othella and I had a bed. There was a stove on one side of the room where we did what little cooking there was. The floors were caked with dirt. No matter how much we scrubbed, the dirt remained. No matter how we cleaned and tried to neaten things up, the room still looked dirty. I never invited anyone up to see me because I was too ashamed.

2

Bal Nègre, one of Dunham's spectacular revues, opened in Philadelphia. After we had gotten the show together, our lives were going along in ordinary fashion when opening night became a little more jumbled than usual because our stage manager disappeared. We learned later he was stricken with a heart attack, which was not surprising with all the voodoo dancing, the screaming of the chants, and the frenzy we got into while performing, each trying to outdo the other.

We all lived in a bed of tension and intrigue. Who was doing what to whom and why? We all talked about each other to each other, searching for a better recognition of ourselves in the eyes of one another. We could not make up our minds whether we should like or hate each other. We wanted to like, but the constant pressure of insecurity kept us from liking others or ourselves. We constantly rebelled against being just another one of the crowd. We hated what we were but we loved it too, for the Dunham company meant something in many ways. It stood for progress for the Negro, a step forward in the eyes of every audience that saw us. We gave better understanding of ourselves to the rest of the world. We stood for a great many things that could never be put into words.

Katherine Dunham had created a better world for many of us, at the same time making the path easier for those who had guts enough to follow. I wanted to talk to her many times—ask questions, say what I felt to her, but I was afraid to get too close. She was not the kind of person one walks right up to and buttonholes. I couldn't really reach her, but I got sensitivity from her. A spiritual kind of feeling, like a wave being received, but uneven. Our communication was always rather rough. When I got a warm word from her, it was a rare one. Every day someone got the butt. When my turns came, usually she'd just look at me and laugh coyly. I couldn't tell whether my whole body was all wrong for dancing, my rear end too big, or what. Then one day it all came out. "You'll never be a good dancer," she said. "You have too much excess baggage." She was looking at my breasts. As the company snickered, I felt so small that I started crying.

"Why did you take me for a dancer then?" I said. "You knew what I looked like before I joined the company." I don't remember her answer but I left the room to pout while the class continued.

I had been with the company for about a year before our engagement in Philadelphia. One night I was standing in the wings, waiting to go on, when I noticed a husky, brown-haired man walk across the stage, checking lights. "I've never seen him before," I thought.

He came off on my side of the stage. Miss Dunham's secretary was standing there when I asked, "Who's that?" in a whisper. Before she could answer, I was on stage, disciplining my feet to the beat of the rumba music. I had forgotten the husky man when I came off, so I did not think about him. I saw him again a few days before we left.

I don't remember how he went about it exactly, but one of the musicians called one of the girls one night to ask her for a date and told her to bring me. When I got to the meeting place, he was there too. It was all very casual, but we started having sandwiches and coffee, then lunch, together. Then dinner—until we fought about the breakfasts.

A sandwich grew into champagne and caviar—with a few bottles of beer in between. It takes some time to down me, but once I'm down, it takes a mule to put me straight again. I knew nothing about him really—just that he was an expert electrician and was very good at his work. "So young," I thought, "to be doing that." I was about seventeen at the time. He was about twenty. The show traveled for six months. By the time we got back to New York, we were deep in caviar.

When we got back to New York, there was discussion about the show going on to Mexico. Sure enough, after rehearsing in New York for a couple of months, we all got on a train to Mexico. It was the first time in my life I had traveled such a great distance at one time. Four days, I think it was. Charlie woke me in the mornings, gave me little signals all day long that I was on his mind. Some little look or sign, when he was reading or playing cards or just sitting. Now and then he'd look up, catch my eye, and go back to what he was doing.

I was so happy because of this wonderful thing that had happened to me I couldn't really talk about it. I couldn't tell him how I felt. There were no words for it. I remember trying to once. He put his fingers over my mouth, saying, "I know." I loved him more for that.

We had a kind of sensitivity about each other that was frightening. A touch, a look, a movement, a silence, told all we felt. The company may have had ideas about us, but they did not really know. He and I would sit on the back of the train, watching the desert float beneath us until the sky turned to pastel colors and then cloaked itself with night.

Each moment grew into a more beautiful one, until our happiness was seeping out of us. I smiled at anything and angered at nothing—only that sleep took us away from each other. Night, I began to loathe the night, but I was grateful that I had tomorrow to look forward to. Each day on the train was about the same.

It was summer in Mexico, so we did a lot of sight-seeing after the show was well on its way. We were to be there for at least two months. Charlie and I were inseparable. If I went somewhere without him, he was lonely. If he was gone for any length of time, I started to fret. But I don't think anyone had any idea how much we cared for each other.

I remember we went to a party one night with the rest of the company. As usual, everybody in the show had to perform. When my turn came, I couldn't refuse very well because everyone else had done his part. "Sing 'Babalu,' " they yelled. I walked into the middle of the floor and sang "Babalu," which was really the only thing I could do at that time, other than some other Spanish songs. When I finished my song, a number of Mexicans came over to congratulate me on my interpretation of a Cuban song—asking if I was Cuban. I became entangled with a number of people, answering their questions, but tried to capture the eye of my lover. I must have been held up for about fifteen minutes or so. When I freed myself, I noticed he had left the room.

I went to look for him in the bar, but I was only confronted by the Dunham dancers. Walking in the garden with no sight of him, I was gradually becoming heartsick. Some time had passed when I noticed a figure walking alone down the path through the garden. I sat on a bench, hoping. When he got near, I heard, "So you finally got away?"

"Where have you been?" I asked.

"Walking."

"Why?"

"Lonely."

"Lonely?"

"Yes."

"Well, I'm here."

"No, you weren't."

"I've been here all the time."

"Not with all those people around you."

"Well, I won't do it anymore."

"I don't mean that. I mean I hate people to touch you. I don't want any hands on you." He stopped, sat down next to me. He took my hands. Holding them tight, he said, "I love you so much it scares me."

The joy swelled up inside of me like a balloon just before it bursts, as his strong manly arms took me to him. The dew kissed our bodies as we clung to each other. The scent of flowers floated in the breeze. The Mexican wind pulled us closer, but discreetly. Can it be that heaven is so wonderful? We returned to the house after a while, took our belongings, gave our thanks, and said good night—with the thought in mind that someday we must live like this.

Some nights Charlie and I would get in a taxi and ride through the Mexican woods—getting out to run through the grass like two younguns, sharing our love with the trees, tumbling over the small bushes and wallowing in the dirt, laughing uncontrollably with the wind as it swept up our joy and spread it like the seeds of wild flowers.

We'd lie in the sand and count the stars: he loves me, he loves me not, he loves me. . . . In silent companionship we'd lie until the dawn. Without a word, we'd wipe our hands of the mist and return to our hotel.

Every day we ate breakfast on the roof of our abode, then made our daily visits to the city. Dinner we'd have at our usual spot, and supper was usually with the gang. We were content just being together, strolling along the streets, often with not a word—just being together.

Then the day came—the end of our engagement in Mexico. A company meeting was called to find out what we wanted to do: stay in Mexico, where we could live cheaper, and rehearse until our picture commitment in Hollywood, or return to the States and wait, or what.

With the exception of a few, the company decided to stay in Mexico, as Miss Dunham had made arrangements for the girls to have a house. The boys could stay at their hotels, with expenses paid by Miss Dunham.

"It would be fun," I thought, as I looked at Charlie. I knew he would not want to stay, doing nothing. "But if he does not stay, I will return with him." My mind was frantic. Patiently I waited for the meeting to end so that could make my decision with him. His face did not have a happy expression. He was thinking desperately. I sensed his worry—maybe I could persuade him to get a job here. I began to invent possibilities, knowing none of them would work. The meeting came to a halt, with all of us having a day or two to make up our minds. I knew by Charlie's expression he would not stay, but maybe—

We walked home that night from the theater, he and I in our secret mood. When we reached our hotel, I went to my room, he to his. I sat on my bed, waiting for a sign.

"Are you going to stay?" he asked, standing in the doorway of my room. He stood there with both hands in his pockets, waiting for the answer.

"Are you?" I asked.

"For three months? Doing nothing?"

"That isn't very long." I fumbled.

"I have to do something. I just can't sit around and waste three months just like that." He moved around the room. I could see he was more than annoyed. I had no idea it would upset him as much as this. He looked at me, straight in the eyes, with fear in the words. "Are you going to stay?"

"I don't know. I'm waiting for you to decide for me, I suppose. Of course I don't want to stay unless you do. But if I go to New York

I'll have to work too, because I have no money. If I stay here with the company I won't need any. There is no point in us both starving to death in New York."

"Then you mean you want to stay?"

"I don't care what we do, stay or not. Whatever you say, Charlie, but I want us both to stay."

"I can't."

"Why not?"

"I just can't. I must work, three months—"

"Why are you so concerned about working? Three months isn't long. You should have enough money saved from the job to take a vacation. It won't cost you anything to live. We can have lots of fun without money. The house Miss Dunham has for us is in the country—we'll meet each other every day. We don't need money—" I held his head against my breasts, trying to convince him we should have fun just living.

His hands around my waist tightened as his body quivered—my heart thumped heavily. He was crying . . . I held on to him, ashamed to look at his face. I did not want to see him cry. I did not know how to treat this situation. He had never done this before. What does a woman do when a man cries? I felt helpless and stupid. I wanted to pull away from him. pretend this had never happened. I could only hold tighter, thankful for a love strong enough to bring tears. My heart began to swell with the joy of love.

"I don't ever want to lose you, Kitten," he whispered. I kissed his hair. He held tight. I began to laugh. Then he chuckled. My heart went on swelling. Our eyes met. I cried. When love beckons, follow it, and I followed.

We went to sleep with our decision undecided. The following day at breakfast, the conversation started again.

"Are you going to meet the company in Hollywood, Charlie, if you return to New York?"

"I would like to, but I cannot get work at the studios. I've asked already."

"Maybe you could get a job out there anyway."

"It would be hard. I don't know anyone there."

"We will know people after we get there. I can introduce you to everyone I meet, and you can take it from there."

"Yeah, I could. I've always wanted to live in California."

He thought about it for a while, then said, "How will I get there? I can't ask my dad for the fare. He's done too much for me now. I don't have any money at all."

"If I stay here for three months, go to Hollywood, do the picture, and so forth, I could send you the fare," I said.

"No, that isn't right. You can't do that," he fussed.

"Why can't I?"

"Because it isn't . . ." He paused, looked into my eyes, and finished with "I love you."

"I love you too."

A few days after the show closed, he left for New York. We didn't say a word to each other in the cab, while it toddled to the airport. I looked out of one window while he looked out of the other—too sensitive to touch, too lost in our misery to find comforting words. At the airport, he walked to and fro, waiting for the plane to leave. He never looked at me directly, just glanced toward me once in a while. I remembered all the wonderful moments we had had. Will they be renewed? Will he remain as much in love as he is now? Will someone else claim him? My heart begged for his love to remain here in Mexico with me.

I was startled by the call to the passengers to board the plane for New York. For a moment we stood face to face, glaring our love into each other's eyes as the passengers pushed their way past us. He kissed me lightly on the cheek, turned, and quickened his steps almost into a run. He walked through the ticket gate without looking back and was lost in the crowd. I stood like a motherless child, watching until the heavens opened up and engulfed the plane.

The little hotel was not the same anymore. This was the first time I had walked through these doors alone. The lobby was cold. The chairs looked ugly, the walls were mean, the elevator suddenly showed its age, the room that I had adored I suddenly hated, the old-fashioned telephone that was so unique was now impractical—I loathed everything I touched. I took a shower to wash away my misery—misery, I glorified in it. It was the kind of misery that made me realize that I was alive, young, and a woman.

3

Gloria Mitchell came over to help me pack for our move into the little house Miss Dunham had rented out in Villa Obregón, about a half hour from the city. It contained three bedrooms, a large living room, kitchen, and bath.

Othella and Dolores took the bedroom opening onto the bricked yard. Greenery grew up the brick wall separating the house from the dirt road. Jackie and I had the bedroom with a window facing the dirt road. Lucille and Ritchie had the upstairs room.

The kitchen was not a very large one but we liked it. Lucille was the head of the family. She was the cook and overseer of all. Each of us had our chores of cleaning up or taking turns for the day's shopping. We had a budget of twenty-five dollars a week for food, which meant we had to spend wisely, even though in Mexico this was quite a lot of money. A Mexican family of six could live on this for about a month, if not longer.

Every morning we'd awake at ten and be ready for class and rehearsals at eleven. After a month or so we had gotten a little tired of our regular diet of plain meat and vegetables. We longed for something a little different, but we could not afford to be in any way extravagant.

What shall we have today to make our feast a little more interesting? It was Sunday; something special should be eaten on Sunday.

Someone had given me a little black pointer dog that we named Babalu. He was quite a hunter. He and I were sitting in the yard when out of the rain pipe from under the wall came a young pullet. It must have gotten lost from the rest of the chickens. It was in search of its playmates. Babalu sat up straight, in wonder of this lone creature. At first I thought I should shoo it out through the gate, but hunger brought the taste of fried chicken to my tongue. I stood up with Babalu at my toes. We both stared at the little strayer, who did not know where to turn. It stared back at us.

"Get him, Babalu," I whispered. The dog darted forth, leaping with joy at the chance. The chicken fluttered about the yard, with wings half spread, hoping for strength to scale the wall. The dog had it in no time. Just as I picked it up, another little stranger peeked in through the rain pipe to see what was happening to its fellow, who was screeching its death call. Not having sense enough to turn around and flee for dear life, the senseless fowl walked right into my hands. Between Babalu and myself, we made a pretty good team of hunters.

The kids screamed with excitement when I walked into the house with our supper. "Kitty, where did you get those? How did you catch them? Did someone give them to you?"

"No," I said.

"Oh, you little devil," they yelled.

Laughter went through the girls, as I said, "Well, here's our something special."

"Who's going to take the job of killing them?" asked Lucille.

The girls hushed, as the horrible thought struck their minds. I looked from girl to girl, then said, "I will. I know how to do it."

I went out in back of the house, took one chicken in my hand while Dolores held the other. With its head gripped tight, I began to twirl its body around as fast as I could, in order to break its neck. I began to feel sorry for this helpless little creature. How can I be so cruel as to wring its neck! "Maybe we should only have one and let the other one go," I said to Dolores, whose head was turned in the opposite direction.

"One won't be enough, silly. They are too small," she chirped. "Go on, you caught them. Finish the job."

"I can't." My eyes began to water as I looked at the half-broken neck. "You walked right into my lap," I said, consoling myself. "If it was not meant to be this way, you would not have found your way through that rain pipe. Who ever heard of a chicken walking through a rain pipe? One of you is just as stupid as the other, so I have no choice but to do my duty as a hungry human being. Off with your heads."

But it was not that easy—the head would not be removed from the body. I pulled and pulled, getting sicker by the minute, hoping each pull would be the last, but the devil himself was in this doggone chicken, keeping it alive to torture me.

The skin of its neck finally broke. Then I really got sick. I wanted to drop the whole thing, put its neck back, forget this ever happened. But I had to go through with it.

The neck was broken at last. The chicken flopped along the ground. I got a butcher knife from the kitchen to disconnect the head from the body, so that it would bleed freely. I remembered you had to do this so that the blood did not spoil the meat or something. The knife was dull, which meant I had to saw the head off. My body shivered uncontrollably as I went about my murdering. I thought of the men whose job it was to bring the hatchet down on the necks of queens. They must have been without souls—or have died a thousand deaths along with the victims.

Dolores handed me the second one, to be slaughtered as madly as I did the first. I bravely took hold of it, laid its head on a rock, and chopped away at its tiny neck, hoping to destroy this one faster. Whack! The head did not fly off as I expected. The knife was too dull. In my disappointment and sickness, I cried, "I can't go through with this one."

Dolores finished the job. I went into the kitchen, put on the water to boil, and smoked a cigarette to calm my nerves. By dinnertime, I was myself again as I bit into the tender meat of a young stray chicken.

Sundays the girls usually went with friends from town to the bullfights, which were terribly exciting. I had gone to one my very first day in Mexico, which we were told not to do because the change of altitude could be dangerous. No alcohol or excitement, we were told. Well, who can refrain from doing something of this sort when told not to? Especially me, whose curiosity is constantly driving me.

I remember how anxious I was to get into the arena and fight the bull, how vicious the people looked around me. How bloodthirsty they all seemed. How sensuous to see blood on the sand. At the beginning of the affair, I missed half of the first fight because I was so busy watching the faces of the spectators. They sat with their fingers in their mouths, biting their nails. Tension was everywhere. I could see it in their faces. I could not understand, or maybe I could, why the arena was so packed by people who could barely afford bread for the table, milk for the children, or shoes for their feet. I thought, maybe they are not an Mexicans—but the majority of them were.

Since we were not supposed to exert ourselves in any way, I tried to keep myself as complacent as possible. But it was a day to remember. When I went to rehearsal that evening, I found out why we had been told not to tire ourselves in any way. The excitement had worn me to a frazzle. I could barely pick my feet up from the floor.

On Saturday nights we gave parties. All of our friends would drive out from the city, loaded down with food and drink. Being faithful to my soulmate, I could not find any interest in anyone else. I felt there was no one who could take his place. Most of the time I stayed in my room or sat in front of the fireplace, moping and panting from loneliness. In my room I could hear the music they played on the phonograph. The rhythmic tunes stirred my loneliness. The slow soft ones melted me to tears. Sometimes I would join the fun and have a swallow or two of tequila, but this usually made me so depressed that I thought I would go mad if I kept it up.

I used to receive a letter from Charlie every day. I lived by the words of these letters. I'd go to bed at night with the day's words on my mind, thinking of what the next day's letter would bring. Each night, faithfully, I would write my daily letter of events.

One day a letter came saying he was on his way back. I glowed with absolute, exhausting happiness. Only a week to wait.

That evening I primped as much as I could, made over one of my shabby dresses as best I could, borrowed cab fare to go to the airport—to meet him. He did not arrive on the plane the letter had mentioned. I walked the airport grounds for an hour before I decided to go back home. Maybe he was not coming. I was furious by the time I got to the house. Why did he disappoint me so?

I was too hurt to make excuses for him, to think maybe he might have had to take another flight for some reason. When I reached the house, our usual Saturday party had begun. The house was full of people. I went directly to my room, as solemn as a preacher. I would not be so consoled.

"Charlie!" I heard his name. He was here. I was too amazed to move. "Kitty, Charlie is here," someone screamed from the living room.

I sat firmly on my bed. "If he wants me let him come and get me," I murmured to myself.

The door opened. He stood in the doorway for a minute or so before plunging forward to take me in his arms. "Oh, Kitten, how I've missed you!" In his strong arms I felt like a doll being squeezed.

When he finally let go of me, the air rushed into my lungs bringing the precious joy of life.

Charlie got himself a room in town and we met every day after my rehearsals. He and I would walk through Obregón Park for hours, mostly in silence, until the hour for sleep arrived. Then he would return to the city.

There was a monument to General Obregón in the park in which we walked. The monument contained the hand of the General, who was a great asset to Mexico during the revolution. He had a powerful left hand, the saying went. He could shoot a peanut from the head of an elephant five miles away, went the saying. His left hand was everyone's envy. It was the strength of Mexico. No one dared challenge Obregón's left hand.

One day I went into the monument to see Obregón's left hand. It was encased in a large jar of alcohol for posterity to admire, this hand of strength and beauty. The idea alone was horrifying to me, but I was curious. It was even more horrifying to discover that someone had made a mistake and preserved the right hand instead of the left. I stayed inside the tomb for half an hour comparing hands—left against the right, right against the left, convincing myself that I had made no mistake. The mistake was in the jar.

After a week or so, Charlie told me he could not find a job with the utility company which had promised him a position. I didn't care if he worked or not, as long as we were together, but he worried about this more than was comfortable from my point of view. He began to investigate every possibility of obtaining work in Mexico. At the end of the day, he would tell me what the possibilities were.

About a week after Charlie returned, he came out to the village two hours before the usual time. I was standing just outside of the gate, during a rehearsal break, when I saw him walking down the little country road to the house. In surprise my shoeless feet bit the dirt to greet him. I ran into his arms, almost throwing him off balance, expecting him to be overjoyed at my reception. His arms were weak as they caught my scarcely dressed body.

"Hi, Charlie. You're early."

"I know."

"What's up? Get lonesome for me?"

"Yeah." He was not himself. He was tense and uncomfortable. "How much time do you have?"

"Oh, I don't know. We just broke, maybe half an hour."

"I have to tell you something. Let's walk." He strolled along with his hands in his pants pockets, kicking the dirt with his feet. "I can't meet you tonight."

"Why not?"

"I have to go to the airport."

"The airport—what for?"

"I have to meet someone."

This someone struck me into stupidity. The strangeness of this someone could not settle lightly in my mind. This someone had a special kind of meaning. I did not want to hear who this someone was. But I had no choice. I went on to ask who this someone was.

His back was turned to me, his head was bent. I could hardly hear the mumbled sound of—"My fiancée."

I swayed from the shock of the words that seeped through to my brain and stopped. It took some time for me to react. I thought of all kinds of meanings for the word "fiancée." Maybe it doesn't mean what I thought it meant. There must be at least two meanings for the same sound. I held on to his arm to brace myself when I asked, "What did—you—say?"

"I wanted to tell you before but I couldn't. I thought I'd wait until I made up my mind to break it off."

I felt a terrible hatred for myself. I had given all there was to give. Flesh for flesh, yet separate hearts. Now I know why he felt such a concern for work. The word "fiancée" was between us.

Now she was here. Why? She had become suspicious. Charlie had phoned his parents that morning. When he asked about her, she had taken a plane to Mexico City.

"When did you think of breaking off your engagement, Charlie, before or after me?"

He turned to me. "Before."

I did not believe him. I could not look at him anymore. I could not stand next to him or talk or breathe the same air with him anymore. My feet moved as though paralysis crept up my legs. As I moved slowly toward the house, my pace turned to a run halfway there.

If I could have cried, I would have felt better, I knew, but I could not. I went back to rehearsal as though I was the happiest kid alive. No one knew. No one suspected that only half of me was the figure in front in the movement of the dance. That night, as I looked at the ceiling from my bed, I prayed for strength.

Charlie did not come to see me for a couple of days after his fiancée arrived. I felt very inadequate as a woman, unattractive, unwanted. After three or four days of absolute loneliness, I decided to go to the city for dinner. An excuse to catch a glimpse of him, if I was lucky.

I knew he would eat in the place we used to eat in because he liked it so much and because it was the only place to get good American food.

Jackie and I took a cab to my haunting grounds. We waited in line at the door for a table, while I combed the place for the sight of him. Jackie suspected nothing until she heard me ask the head waiter if he had come in yet.

"Is he still here?" Jackie asked.

I pretended not to hear her, as the waiter led us to a table. I made up my mind to sit here until he showed up. I knew he would be coming in soon, if at all. . . . Suppose he doesn't, I thought. Then I'll come back tomorrow and every day until he does. She will be with him, I know. I want to see what she looks like. If she's small, pretty, ugly, or what not. I want to see his face when he sees mine, just to see what he will do, if he's a coward and pretends he does not see me or if he will acknowledge me, and what will she do; probably pretend she knows nothing. . . .

It must have been at least an hour and a half before I decided to give up. We had eaten a full dinner, ending with ice cream, paid the bill, and started to walk out of the door as he walked into the restaurant, with her slightly in front of him. He did exactly what I expected him to do—looked right into my eyes and cringed. He thought she would see me, but she did not.

My eyes followed them, him not letting on that anything was wrong, until my heart finally burst into tears. I got into a cab and returned to the villa, comforted by Jackie, who finally understood what was wrong.

I went on about my affairs and the dancing without seeing him, until one evening he came to tell me he had to return to America. We had very little to say to each other. The situation was too dramatic. He swore again he was going to break his engagement. I told him I did not want to be responsible. He swore again. He asked me to bear with him. He had decided before I was in the picture. He had become engaged out of loneliness and with the encouragement of his family and hers, and without finding out if he was really in love or not.

True or not, I believed him. With this belief, I made secret plans on how to help him get to California.

4

A few weeks after this, the company was offered an engagement at Ciro's in Mexico City. We were all glad to get the job, though Miss Dunham could only afford to pay us thirty-five or forty dollars a week, depending on our positions in the company. I moved into the city to a small hotel which cost me ten dollars a week.

Our engagement at Ciro's lasted two months.

The second day, I was standing in the lobby of the hotel in which Ciro's is located, waiting for Gloria, when a very handsome Mexican came up to me, took off his hat with greetings of the evening in excellent English.

Not knowing exactly what to do, acknowledge the greeting or ignore him, I sort of did nothing but at the same time gave him that look of "Keep trying." He looked awfully familiar to me. I wanted him to get acquainted but I was afraid to cheapen myself and look like a pickup.

He went over to the desk where everyone scraped the floor with salutations to him. I was sorry not to know him. Finally he came up to me again. "Would you like to join me for a drink, Senorita?"

"No, thank you. I do not drink."

"Would you like something to eat maybe, no?" I was hungry and this was a way to get a free meal. But how could I just walk off with a stranger? I looked at him, smiling with unsureness. "Why don't you just join me, and I will lead the way. Maybe something will strike your fancy later, eh?"

"I'm sorry but I'm waiting for a girlfriend who should be here any minute."

"Oh, then, she may join us too." He must be on the level, if Gloria can come, I thought.

"Well—I—Gloria!" She walked up to us. "Gloria, this is—" He interrupted. "I tell you what, there is a little party being given here by a friend of mine who's a dancer. Would you like to go up with me? His name's R—."

"I know him very well," said Gloria. "Sure, come on." We three got on the elevator which, after mounting seven or eight floors, opened into a studio containing several well-dressed couples dancing to rumba records being played on a phonograph in a corner.

Mr. R— was running from couple to couple, making exclamations. "Do not shake the buttocks so. Move from the knee. No, no, no, that is not the rumba. That is the two-step." He got a glimpse of us waiting for his attention. "Hello, please come in, come in."

Mr. R— greeted the man who had picked us up, "I'm so glad to see you. Where have you been?" But he turned quickly to a couple who were dancing past us. "No, no," he exclaimed. "The rumba is not a fight between husband and wife. You make love with it, like this."

He pushed the man aside, took the woman in his arms, and went gliding across the floor with bent knees, pushing his buttocks from side to side in an exaggerated motion. "You see how the buttocks follow the movement of the knee?" he said. "Very easy, very simple—not complicated at all. Now you do it."

The two fumbled, trying to get the simple but complicated step. "One, two, three, four," went the teacher. I thought it very funny for an American to be teaching Mexicans how to rumba, but that was life, I supposed.

Then Mr. R— came back to us. We had made ourselves at home, with a coke for me, scotch and soda for Mr. Whomever. Gloria had something like tequila and lemon. Mr. R— whispered to us, "These people don't know their behinds from their faces, but it's a buck." He shrugged his shoulders. "Good thing this is only temporary. I'm going home in a couple of months. New York. Can't wait."

"What's the matter, don't you like Mexico?" Mr. Whatever asked.

"Yes, but only if I can loaf."

Mr. Whozit turned to me. "By the way, this is Eartha Kitt and this is—what did you say your name was?"

"Gloria Mitchell."

How did he know my name? I thought. He must have seen our show.

"What are you doing in Mexico City?" asked Mr. R—.

"Loafing," Mr. Whatzit said.

"I thought you were on location somewhere, finishing your picture." *Finishing your picture!* He's a movie star—but which one? I wandered over to Gloria, who was carrying on a conversation with one of the students of the rumba, but Gloria was deeply engrossed.

Who was this man? If I could only recall where I had seen the face before. It had something to do with sadness, I knew. I returned to the two, who were still talking. Maybe I'd get a clue soon if Mr. R— kept asking about his films. Finally I heard it. I knew who this was. I looked at him more closely. Yes, the same face, a little older, but the same face. A little less hair now, but the same face—what a body he had! I had fallen in love with him when I saw the film and here he stood in front of me.

I recalled the feeling I had for him when I saw him on the screen. His eyes fascinated me, the pathetic expression on his face, the sadness of his mouth. The love he had for the girl, the hurt he felt when she was stoned to death at the end of the picture. This was the man who picked me up in the lobby of the Hotel de la Reforma, who asked me to join him in a drink, who was now standing face to face with me—Pedro Armendariz.

I said nothing for the rest of the evening—I just basked in his presence. After the party, we, along with Mr. R.—, went to a club to see the last show. We had sandwiches and drinks. Pedro was greeted warmly by all, especially the female species. After the show, he took us to our little hotel. As he left me at the door, he said, "I'll come by tomorrow at four to pick you up for dinner."

I went to sleep a happy little soul. This might be the way to get Charlie out of my system. The next afternoon I awoke around two-thirty, ordered coffee and toast, which was horrible, took a shower, patiently dressed, fixed my hair—which in itself took a half hour to get that satisfied look, and wondered if he really meant what he said about coming for me at four.

The more I thought of the improbability of his coming for little ol' me, the more I talked myself out of waiting. It was three forty-five when I went to Gloria's room to see if she was there. She was not. I went downstairs to the lobby of the hotel. I forced a conversation with one of the desk men to kill time. Ten minutes of four. I knew he wasn't coming. . . . Why should I wait for him to make a fool of me with disappointment? I won't wait any longer—it's five minutes to four. If I wait until four and he does not come, I'll be hurt. I must save myself from that. I'll leave. I'll give myself the satisfaction of not being disappointed.

"If anyone wants me, I'll be at the Hotel de la Reforma on the roof," I said to the clerk. I walked out of the door on my way to the hotel in which we worked, glancing back to see if his car was pulling up. No car—no Pedro.

I reached my destination around four-thirty, window-shopping on my way. I was sure I would never see him again. When I got to the hotel, I asked if there were any messages for me. There was none. I knew he was lying, I thought. I went up on the roof where our dressing room was, took a book, and read until the rest of the company started arriving.

The show went on as usual, and, when I sang my song, my eyes searched for Pedro in the audience. He was not to be seen. After the shows were over, Gloria and I got dressed and headed for home. Just outside of the hotel, Pedro walked up to me, saying, "Why did you not wait for me? I was only five minutes late."

I continued to see Pedro for the duration of our Mexico stay. He was always a gentleman and a great lover of life. He had a friend who was a cinema director. When the two of them got together, it was fun, each competing with the other to tell the biggest story. They had a bond between them that always kept them together, a kind of mental telepathy that sensed danger for the other. Whenever one was in trouble, no matter where the other might be, the telepathic contact was strong enough to bring the other to the rescue.

Sometimes Pedro took us to fascinating places. For instance, one evening we went to a side-road bar. It was much the same as any other Mexican bar from the front, but the back door led to a secluded alcove of tiny houses covered with clusters of trees and flowers. The cabins could not be seen from the road or from the bar. They were lit by candlelight. The murals on the walls were of Mexican peasant life, beautifully painted. The curtains were Mexican prints. The floors were stone. The little houses contained one room with a settee, two chairs, a table in the middle of the floor. There were rugs made of rope on the floor, pillows all over the place, a tiny fireplace, and a heavenly atmosphere. The sun had gone down by the time we got to this secret rendezvous.

Pedro and I sat on the floor of the cabin around the table as a pretty waitress served us tequila and tortillas. From the window I could hear the serenaders who usually traveled in fours from bar to bar, playing their guitars and singing. The sound of the guitars came closer and closer until they were upon us. They joined us in the drinking between songs.

Pedro would throw them coins and they would laugh. They left after four or five songs. We finished our drinks of tequila, licking the salt from between thumb and index finger and sucking on a lemon to encourage or kill the taste of the Mexican liquor.

I was slightly tipsy as we joined the others in the main bar. It was quite an experience, being with such a handsome, sensuous man who maintained his distance. I feared him not thereafter. The others teased me on the way home, for I was always the one to frown on alcohol. All I ever needed was one drink to finish me off.

The next day Pedro picked me up early in the afternoon to see a film of his that was playing in town, La Perla. The experience of seeing the man sitting next to me on the screen was an inexpressible one. The story was about a fisherman in a tiny village on the sea who one day found a pearl and found the way at last to call his soul his own. The villagers were extreme paupers. Their only means of survival was from the sea. He wanted to run away. Another world would be different.

He did not realize that the world is the same no matter what part of it one is in. Where riches are concerned, people have a very bad habit of wanting too much or not enough. We have never mastered the happy medium of being satisfied with enough. Enough never is enough. We have forgotten how to live with God. Rather we have forced God to live with us.

My thoughts at this time of my life were not very mature. I felt insincere in practically everything I did, for I did not have a complete understanding of myself or life. My confused mind absorbed confused thoughts. I lived negatively. Maybe that is the reason why this film stuck in my mind, not so much that Pedro was in it, but the story itself. The transition of the soul into ugliness when it realizes that riches can buy anything.

One morning in Mexico City I was taken to church. Not being Catholic, I was more or less interested in how the people of a foreign country, as well as another religion, went about worshipping my God. The church was rather small, but immaculate. The benches were worn, the floor was of dirt, the stained windows were bright with the morning light.

We walked down the aisle to the front where the natives gathered in prayer, kneeling, some standing, some sitting. The thing that struck me most was that, poor as the people were, they came and graciously put their hard-earned pesos in the plate at the altar.

I wondered if this was what God wanted. Was he grateful for this much generosity or would he be more grateful if they had kept their pesos for food? So many things I did not understand when I thought of God as a man who guided us from day to day. I thought of him as goodness without an evil thought.

5

When our Ciro's engagement ended, we left Mexico City and went to Hollywood where we were to take part in making a movie. Hollywood. The glamour world.

We were pretty tired after three days of travel and we had to look for a place to stay. We were told we could not live in hotels like other people, so we took up with private families.

Richie and Dolores knew a woman who catered to entertainers. They thought I could get a room, too, which I did, sleeping on the couch in the living room. But the woman found out what I looked like three days later when she got a good look at me and said, "Out!" in no uncertain terms, me being of lighter complexion.

I had a strong fear of Hollywood. At the same time, it was fascinating. I had dreamed of becoming a part of this kind of world, but actually being here mingling with the stars was hard to accept as real. I was still a child, having an extremely vivid dream.

A few days after our arrival, Miss Dunham called to take me out to the studio with her, along with Jessie Hawkins. We drove into the lot of Universal-International, parked our car among the others, and started to what turned out to be the director's office. Having my coat on my arm, I thought it too hot to be bothered, so I ran back and threw my coat in the car.

I sat in a chair with my legs crossed, next to Miss Dunham, as a virile, curly-haired, handsome, careless, quiet-looking dog came into the little cabin, followed by a master with the same make-up, both marvelous to look at.

The moment he walked into the room, our eyes met. He did not move his eyes, though he talked to everyone in the room. This went on for such a long time that I became uncomfortable, though I liked the way he looked at me. No one had ever quite looked at me like that before.

—He undressed me, caressed me, made love to me, hugged me, penetrated my womanliness, and made me so completely aware of my sex that, at that moment, we were in love, not with each other, but with man and woman. . . .

I played with the dog, while the business transaction was going on. Miss Dunham wanted them to do something special with Jessie and me, but it was later ruled out. When I got home that evening I found I had forgotten my coat. When I saw Miss Dunham the following day it was not in her car. I had obviously thrown it in another car. It was not until the day we started work at the studio that I learned I had thrown my coat in the car that belonged to him, of all people. Not knowing to whom it belonged, he had thrown it in the back seat, thinking someone would come in search of it.

When I did, after the day's work, John took me to dinner across the street from the studio. The restaurant had the best steak I had ever eaten. He didn't know it and of course I did not let on to that. It was the biggest piece of meat I had ever seen on a plate. The salad was something out of this world too.

He ordered wine, red wine. I sipped a small glass to stimulate my appetite, as he suggested. It was stimulated, all right. I ate like two pigs—I could hardly move when it was time to go. He was too busy talking to his friends to notice, but I was having problems, not knowing exactly how to go about things. Shall I put the salad on the plate with the steak—shall I drink the wine first or with the meal? He was gabbing away, while I stuffed myself—thank heavens, he was not watching.

When he finally came to notice me, I stopped everything—he looked at me and smiled. Probably he knew all along what was going on. Without a word, he put on his coat, beckoned me to do the same, and took me home.

I had taken a room on the same street with Dolores and Richie so that they called for me every morning on the way to the streetcar that took us out to Universal City. I did not let on that I had gotten acquainted with him or that we met every day for lunch or for dinner. He never showed any special attention to me on the lot, but, when our eyes met, we knew we were on each other's mind.

The film-making produced a numb kind of feeling in me. I never actually felt I was there completely. In my childhood Shirley Temple had provided my mental image of Hollywood. When I saw her on the screen; I thought of a big beautiful house with dolls in every room, a swimming pool, a chauffeur-driven car, a dog, lawn, lawn, lawn. Shirley must have had a new dress for every hour and ice cream whenever she wanted. I imagined her ordering her chauffeur to take her to the nearest ice cream parlor.

I expected to see movie stars on every corner, but they were not even seen on the lot. When I did see Tony Martin and Peter Lorre, who were in our picture, I was not moved at all, but took everything very naturally as though I had expected all of this to come about. It was just another phase of my dream coming true.

I was excited by all the sets of little cities man had made to portray the stories. I was excited by all the cameras and the many people who worked on one film. I was entranced by the takes and retakes of a scene—or the yelling of "Quiet," "Cut," "Take," "Wrap it up," and so on, but it was a controlled excitement, as though I was storing everything up for the proper moment. I kept my ears and eyes open all the time.

When we were not needed on the set, we went visiting other sets, we saw Deanna Durbin and Vincent Price on the set of *Up in Central Park*, Louis Jourdan and Joan Fontaine on the set of *The Letter*, Edward G. Robinson and Burt Lancaster on the set of *All My Sons*. We went from lot to lot, getting acquainted with everyone to the point that we were being invited to people's cabins for drinks and lunch. Some of these people later became close associates of ours. I can't say Hollywood was what I expected it to be, because I had had no idea what to expect.

There were parties being given all the time, but for some reason I never bothered to participate. Maybe because I did not drink, I saw no reason for going. Besides, having to get up at such early hours, I did not like night life. I always found myself at home at a decent hour.

The wardrobe we had for the picture was rather interesting; since we had to be Arabs, our costumes were a little on the strange side. In one scene we had on fezzes with a shawl effect around our hair, a bolero jacket, and a flare skirt. This was the scene where I made my film debut. It became muddled somewhere along the line in processing the day's work. During the dance, I snapped my fingers in Tony Martin's face and said, "Come on, Pepe." Whereupon he looked at us disgustedly and walked out.

The other sequence we had was a frenzied thing where everyone, including Miss Dunham, went out of his head. I was the second girl from the left, the last to twirl into unconsciousness, falling on top of everyone who had already twirled into unconsciousness and fallen on someone else.

Yvonne De Carlo was the girl who was in love with Pepe, Marta Toren was the girl Pepe falls in love with, Peter Lorre was the Detective, Tommy Gomez was the Inspector. The airplane was the only miscast. This picture made me feel rather important, because everyone got the same salary. For the first time, I did not have to talk my way into a raise; because of a union ruling or something, we got paid $150 a week. With this I opened a bank account and started saving.

A few days after we started on the film, Charlie arrived on the scene. I was as usual very happy to see him. He arrived while I was at the studio and found a reservation I made for him at the hotel. A few days later he moved into a private home nearer me. He was still engaged to marry the family choice.

I had become resigned to the idea of destroying my feeling for this man, but, after being with him a couple of days, I found it was not easy. My incompleteness made me lonely when he was not around, unsatisfied if my questions did not receive the right answers, frustrated when I did not make the right move to make a stronger claim.

I was uneasy because I did not want to be in love with him anymore, but the feeling was too great a satisfaction for me to let it go without a substitute. Selfish of me, but women will be women. Then too perhaps by some chance he would come to a decision and we could have our life together.

He became casual with me in public—as though I was just a friend. There were few or no affectionate scenes of holding hands. I thought, maybe I'm imagining this.

There was always a certain kind of feeling hanging in the air between us. The kind that I had when I was a kid and did something wrong, knowing I was going to get a whipping when my aunt came home. I couldn't think what I had done to deserve it, but whenever I was with Charlie, the feeling was alive. . . . How can I explain I did nothing wrong? besides, I'm a big girl now. You're not supposed to whip me. I have a mind of my own now. Why should I feel guilty of anything?

We were in Hollywood about six weeks and now Charlie was seeing me infrequently. He came to the house one night when I had cooked dinner for the two of us. He ate heartily, drank gluttonously, kissed me coolly on the cheek, complimented me on my cooking, and said, "Let's talk."

A breeze tingled my skin in expectation of "something wrong." He sat me down next to him at the table and said, "I don't think we should see too much of each other here."

"What do you mean?"

"Well, you know how people are, especially out here. I'm trying to get somewhere and so are you, so I think we should be discreet about ourselves."

"You mean we should not be seen in public together?"

"Well—yes."

"How do you intend to manage that?" I asked, practically gritting my teeth from the hurt.

"I'll come to see you whenever I can here. We can meet as usual in our eating place, but you know how people talk. I don't want to ruin my chances of getting a job before I get started."

I looked at the man. After all the joys and self-giving each unto the other, the love, the wonderful love we had, the promises he had made to me, after all this, he wanted me to be a back-street wife. Is he afraid? Of what? Of man, who might tell him what and how and whom to love? Why should he live in fear if he is not guilty of any wrongs? Am I mad to think you are conforming to conformity that is wrong? Am I wrong to want you to fight for what brings you a little happiness, be it black or white or whatnot? Are you afraid to be put against a wall and shot for loving a black woman? Will you be?...

I could not answer the questions in my head; neither could he. I knew and sympathized with what he must have felt to bring himself to tell me this, but how could I show him this thinking was wrong? If he wanted to let me go completely, all right, if he was afraid. But he must not ask me to meet in dark alleys or dingy rooms and hallways to have a little love and then return to the clean "nowrongdoing" outside world of glaring neon signs where man lived in a white world and where blacks huddled in the dark trying to make neon signs of their own.

"I'm sorry, Charlie, but if this is what you want of me, I cannot accept. I can only see you in a light which we both hold the string to, to turn on, to stand in the circle of that light, to see each other as we are—people. I must be free to love. I will not be tied down to hate."

We discussed the point to its exhaustion, until I said good night to him, never giving an inch.

"I don't want to lose you, Kitt. Can't you understand?"

"I understand," I said, "but I will not accept."

He left with his head drooped forward, thinking probably that I would call him later, asking for forgiveness as I usually did when I found I had been a fool about something.

I continued with my studio work, continued to have dinner with John, and did not call Charlie or speak about him to the others. After seven days, I was taken home by John, who said good night in front of my door.

I felt rather strange as John and I stood on the sidewalk chatting. Someone was watching me. That evilness took hold of me, warning me to be careful. Silly, I thought, how one's senses could run away with themselves. Someone was standing behind that tree watching. My ego was flattering itself. Charlie certainly couldn't do a thing like that. Anyway, we were through.

Don't be silly, one does not fall out of love overnight. My inner self talked to me as John held me in his arms, waiting for me to say something. I tried to glance around me to see if I could catch a shadow lurking anywhere, but I could not. "You go right to bed now; don't stay up," John said.

"All right, John. Good night." I didn't want him to go because my instinct told me not to let him go, but my conscious self said I was being silly. I said nothing to John, went into the house and to my room. There was no one in the house but me.

Knock! Knock! Someone was at the door. I knew exactly who it was. I knew he was mad, knew he had seen every move I made. He stood there. "Is this what you have been doing not to be home when I call? This must have been going on for some time."

He snatched me up by the collar of my shirt and threw me on the floor." How dare you make a fool out of me? Who do you think you are? Who is that man who brought you home? Get up off the floor."

I sat on the floor in surprise to have him rough me up this way, something he had never done or dreamed of doing that I could recall. He was like a mad monster, straddling over me, hating me for being a woman.

Shall I cry to keep him from hitting me again, or shall I stand up and take it? To protect myself, I decided to whimper a little. If he feels sorry for me, he'll want to make me feel secure again, to show me how much I love him and need him, to weaken me as a woman, to get me to do his bidding. Or shall I kick him in his groin and make him crawl out my door on his belly?

He dragged me up to my feet and angered me so that I began to fight him like a man. I had struck a right to the jaw, a blow in the abdomen, and was aiming for the left cheek before he got the upper hand. When he was able to control me by throwing me down on the bed and using his body to hold mine steady, my senses calculated themselves when I felt his lips on mine, melting into love.

Everyone seemed to be stirred up these days about something called the world situation. I was not aware of politics enough to know what was going on exactly, and it was all very strange to me.

People talking about what Russia thought or what we thought. I could only get the gist of a lot of this at parties, because no one bothered to discuss politics or Russia or America with me. Not knowing what was going on in the world, I could hardly join in a highly intellectual discussion of world events.

At parties, I was always conscious of not being able to talk on anything except the last dance we learned or how the audience reacted. I was constantly amazed at myself because I had not taught my mind to think enough of me to read the proper books or think there was any more to a newspaper than Dick Tracy and Little Orphan Annie. I always thought of myself as Annie. The harder the life, the easier it was to combat. How would I go about getting out of Annie's situation?

I wanted to know what these people knew who sat around at parties discussing Stalin, Roosevelt, and whomever. I could have found much of this in newspapers, but I was too lazy, I suppose, to read a book from end to end or to be able to understand what I had read. I tried, but it was often useless.

I thought that by going to school one could learn how to think—which is really what school is for, I suppose—but at this late date I was conscious only of what I did not know. When I heard people talking on different subjects that were foreign to me, I was hypnotized by the wonder of their knowledge. One night after we had visited some friends who talked world events the whole evening, I felt very embarrassed because the woman of the house tried to bring me into the conversation by saying, "Don't you think so?" and I was unable to answer her. Others looked at me and smiled, but I was sick from embarrassment. When I got home that night, I cried from lack of knowledge.

I knew what my main problem was, to teach myself how to think, absorb, and retain. Somewhere along the line I had forgotten about all this. I began inquiring about books to read and had them explained to me when I did not understand. I think my greatest asset was I was not afraid to admit I did not know. I found that honesty gave me a leeway to obtaining knowledge.

Charlie would sit for hours explaining the hows, whats, and whys of many things. I could be as ignorant as I really was with him and not be ashamed. I think he really admired me for admitting I did not know. It gave him something to mold, someone he could teach. I had to respect him, look up to him.

I was going to miss all this when there was no more Charlie. After our last violent evening, I had made up my mind the next morning on the studio lot that we had to part. Miss Dunham had said something about Europe, but no one took her seriously, for it seemed too far-fetched. I was hoping it was all true. It would be the perfect way out. Away from him completely, no phone to pick up when I was miserable—an ocean of salt water to wash my veins, cleanse my soul, irrigate my heart.

I said nothing to Charlie about my plan to leave him. As a matter of fact, he was pretty sure we would not get too serious about Europe. He laughed it off and said, "You won't go anyway."

6

When the film was finished, we went into Ciro's in Hollywood for a two-week engagement, where the Dunham troupe was made very proud by the presence of the Hollywood pie crust. The club was filled to capacity every night, and we thought ourselves the hottest things alive. We were proud to be what we were, with no regrets, except when we thought of ourselves as a part of this society. I felt we were infringing on it. I always felt there was an opening somewhere, that all I had to do was find it. The way or the means of this discovery was a mystery I had to solve. I felt that this world of theirs was not afraid of us, but we were afraid of them, that if we showed ourselves on equal terms we might not even be noticed. It would mean understanding, not tolerance. To be tolerated would be worse than nonacceptance.

I wanted the world to understand me in order to accept me. I had no real desire to mingle at society functions or what-nots. To tell the truth, I usually found some nook in a bedroom somewhere at parties and slept until it was time to leave. A strangeness came over me at social gatherings. Why am I here? What purpose do I serve? Whose memory shall I take away with me?

I kept in my head a thought that one day I might come back, meet them face to face, on their level, be able to hold my own. To know and be able to express, to differentiate truth from pretense. To have value for myself and to be able to communicate in order to be understood.

There was so much I had to do. Very often I could only feel it way down deep inside of me. When I thought of me, I thought of many me's—the me's of yesterday, today—and what I was to be tomorrow. There were no words for this, whatever it was; to go on, never looking back. I had no real grasp of what I was aiming at, but the drive, the desire, the go-ahead was there. I often felt as though some power in the air kept pulling me toward it. I was tied to a string that now and then would tug me slightly.

Charlie was not the right direction—I knew it, but at the moment he was love. I had a feeling that the other direction for some reason held great satisfaction, but I would not find love of this kind everywhere. The argument with myself was which was more important. No matter what I was heading for, I knew the search for love would always exist.

When our two weeks at Ciro's came to an end, the Dunham show toured to the coldest and most horrifying of cities. What an impression it made on me! I was ready to leave the moment we arrived. The snow was at least seven feet deep. The icy fingers of Lake Michigan ran up and down my spine. Being a person who hates cold weather, I was prepared to hate Chicago from the start.

As happened in every city we had played, except Mexico, we had to live in segregated parts of town, a great distance from the theater. Reservations were made for us by the company manager who had preceded us. Our hotel was on the South Side, about five to ten miles from downtown. A large chunk of our salary was consumed by trolley car or bus.

After being there a few days, we began to meet people and started to have an enjoyable time. There was one thing about Chicago I loved that January—shoe shopping. I began to get fond of the old icebox. At least the people were friendly, the ones I met.

One night, Gloria, who was rooming with me, asked me if I would like to go out on a blind date. I said okay when Gloria explained the boys were students of medicine and at the same time practicing at some hospital. The doctors were having a little shindig. Having seen the show, her friend wanted her to bring me to the party for his friend.

The party went well. Everyone was pleasant and friendly, everyone had lots to drink and still the party was good fun. The boy whose date I was very nice—intelligent, talked well, a gentleman.

We danced to a phonograph and were very happy. When the party was over, our partners escorted us to a car to take us home. On the way, Gloria's friend said, "Let's go to the hotel of a friend of mine. We can have a few drinks in the room and finish the party up there."

I was not too much for the idea, but I did not want to throw a damper on the rest, so I went along. We got a room and ordered more drinks. The blind date amused me with unfunny jokes until I heard the cry of Gloria who had gone into another room with her date. I sat uncomfortably until I heard a second cry that brought me to my feet and to the door. Knocking nervously, I yelled, "Are you all right?" She mumbled something through the door.

I kept knocking. I thought if I kept annoying them, one of them would open the door. Which worked in due time, but the results were not too comfortable. Gloria's date opened the door, saying, "What's the matter?"

I had walked into the room, hoping to see exactly what I saw and nothing else—Gloria standing in front of the mirror combing her hair. She did not look ruffled but a little frightened.

"Are you ready to go?" I asked.

"Yes."

"What do you mean, go?" the partner asked boisterously. "You're not going anywhere," he yelled. "Sit down." He was getting brutal and I was getting scared. At first I thought this was his sense of humor. He must have been pretending to be a caveman of some kind. I soon found out he was no joker. I felt a blow across my head that blurred my eyes and trickled my face with blood. I felt my head in a state of shock and surprise, not believing this had really happened. Gloria stood in her tracks, not knowing what to do.

My date quickly took me away to another part of the hotel and washed the blood from my face, as Gloria looked on with saddened eyes. On the way to our hotel, my date kept apologizing for his friend, saying he had never seen him in that condition before. Something must have gone wrong, he said, which was no lie.

Dale Wasserman had taken over the stage managing. He had been with the company on and off for many years. He was also personal manager and good friend to Miss Dunham.

By this time we were talking seriously about Europe, and Dale began to prepare everyone with his third degree: "Are you going?" "If not, why not?" "Don't you want to see Europe?" "Don't you realize what an opportunity this is?"

I had decided not to go. I wanted to return to Hollywood. "I don't want to go to London."

"Why not?"

"I want to go back to Hollywood."

"Kitty, be sensible. Come to Europe—you won't regret it."

A word or two from Dale every day made me decide finally it had to be Europe, now or never.

On my return to New York, I accepted my aunt's invitation to stay at home with her. Those ten days brought us close for the first time in our lives. I began to realize she was a warm and sensitive woman, with strength that kept her going though death was in her path.

I learned that she was not afraid of life and the payment for it. She looked to no one for anything, she looked to God for the strength to keep going. She began to love me. She wanted to accept me as completely hers, as though through her womb I was created.

The house was warm. The furniture hugged me when I sat, the bed folded me when I slept, and the kitchen called me with scents of home-cooked food. I had been finally adopted. When I left the house, I could not wait to get back to it again. I had some place to belong. I told her I needed some new clothes and things for my voyage, such as suitcases, slips, and so forth. I had intended to get these things myself, since I had saved a little money, but I came home from rehearsal one day to find she had supplied me with everything I needed.

She showed me everything, piece by piece, saying, "If there is anything you don't like, I can take it back." Because of my excitement, I wanted to talk more and more, to tell her how I had wanted this to happen for a long time, how I had longed for her to show me love.

Instead, I said, "Mother, I started a bank account in Los Angeles. If you want, I can have Miss Dunham send the money to you instead of there."

"Never mind," she said. "I know how you are with money.

It'll never get there."

"But I am saving." I did not have my bankbook to prove it, so I could not make her believe me. She went into her handbag and brought out two tiny card-like envelopes. She opened one little book and showed it to me. Eartha Kitt was at the top of the first page. A few lines down, it gave dates and sums, the last figure being $1,300. The book containing her name came to $2,300.

I felt ill all over. My thoughts went back to the empty ice-boxes—no milk—no shoes on my feet—the shabby clothes she used to wear—the hand-me-downs we both wore from the white world. All this time she must have been putting money aside for me to have when I grew up. "Of course if anything happened to me, all of this, along with the insurance I have taken out, will be yours," she said.

I had a mother again suddenly, but what made her own me? She wanted me home, I felt. She was proud that I had not turned out to be a no-good. The umbilical cord was imaginary but the sensation of a mother was real. I wished we were not going away. Allow me to hold these precious moments a little longer—give me time to thank my God for beauty of emotion.

The day before we were to leave, I called Charlie to tell him I would see him in six months—after our expected stay in London. He begged me not to go, but I had made up my mind. I told him this would give him a chance to decide which woman he was to choose. He was on his own. I was emotionally disturbed after the call, but I knew time would hold hands with me—pro or con.

The next day at eleven, my aunt took me to the S.S. George Washington to join the company. I was proud to strut among the others, saying, "This is my mother." She talked and joked with the other mothers and the company, making me proud to call her mother.

The ship blew its whistle for the warning, "All ashore!" She looked down at me from her strong shoulders and said, "I feel I shall never see you again." My heart swelled as tears fell on her proud cheeks, sad over me for the first time that I could remember. This was the last time she was to see me. We went about our affairs on the boat, such as choosing beds, getting settled. All of the girls were put in one room; so were the boys—in double beds, upper and lower. In no time at all, everyone except me went about getting acquainted.

I lay in my lower bed with no intention of getting up till we reached London, unless of course I was on the verge of starving. I had a lot on my mind and wanted to be alone. The only way to do this was to sleep in order not to hear, see, or be disturbed. This is what I did. When I finally decided to get up, I became terribly seasick and couldn't get up.

The last four days I spent completely in bed, too seasick to care about living or dying. There were times the sea was so rough I thought sure we were goners. My bed leaned so far to the floor I knew the ship must have lain on its side in its own agony.

After seven days we saw the cliffs of Dover that we had heard so much about. I managed to stand on the deck to see if the cliffs were really white. The boat went on to Southampton, England. When we reached Southampton, the boat eased into the harbor, grateful to arrive at last. It seemed as though it, like me, was on its last legs.

Hollywood Mocambo, 1953, in costume and recording

etween takes—recording session

Run-through with Henri Renée

Stills from *New Faces* film

Opening Night, *New Faces*, May 16, 1952, with Franchot Tone and Ronnie Graham

From motion picture, *New Faces*

El Rancho, Las Vegas, 1955

Study by Philippe Halsman

Still from *Mrs. Patterson*

TV rehearsal, 1954

Omnibus' TV *Salome*, December 19[illegible]
(above and below)

Winter 1955, Copa

1954, La Vie en Rose

PART THREE

1

WE GOT off the boat at Southampton with the feeling of Alice in Wonderland. We stood alongside watching the boat unload for a while before claiming our belongings at customs, where they made us open up everything before passing through. The main question was if we were carrying in American cigarettes or food of any kind. One opened carton of cigarettes was allowed, along with five pounds of food.

There were crates and crates of food Miss Dunham had sent on our tickets, for she had been told of the scarcities. We had no idea what we were transporting until we got to customs. For months after that, whenever we saw American canned food we were homesick. A lot of our stuff was given to the British. It was 1948 and they had been short of meats, milk, sugar, coffee, cheese, and whatnot for so long. I saw Miss Dunham give away a few cans and the expression of the receiver's face was worth the trip. These were the times I appreciated my birthright.

When we got to London proper by train, we were met by a gentleman who was to see that we were properly situated. Like a company manager, he had made reservations in private homes for us, as hotels were too expensive.

We were taken to these homes by bus and dropped off. Most of the girls were in one house—three in one room, four in another with a bath on a level between the second and third floors. These places were five pounds a week per person.

None of us was satisfied but we did not know how to find anything else. We all met halfway down the hall, looked at each other, sat on the stairs, and said, "What now?"

Julie had the name of a restaurant that served excellent Jewish food, given to her by her mother. She asked me if I would go with her to have dinner in this restaurant. We had about a pound between us and a few dollars, so we ate the cheapest thing on the menu—matzoth-ball soup. It was here we made up our minds to find an apartment, after spending an hour or so laughing about our lives and how amusing it can be at times.

As luck would have it, Julie asked the owner if he knew of an empty apartment. Much to our surprise, after a phone call, he found one that we could move into the following day. It was at 10 Manchester Square, in a beautiful neighborhood: two bedrooms, a living room with fireplace, a bath large enough for a double bed to fit in, a kitchen, and a telephone. It was expensive. I was only making ninety-five dollars a week. At four dollars to the pound I wound up with about five pounds, after savings deductions, and that usually went into food.

Julie and I had lots of fun housekeeping—I would cook the dinners, she the breakfasts, and we both did the dishes. We were very happy in our little abode. We had our English ration books that entitled us to meat, eggs, cheese, milk, sugar, or anything else that was rationed—including chocolate and other sweets that we usually gave to the English, for neither Julie nor I were candy eaters. We gradually became acquainted with people who helped us by telling us where to buy. We soon felt at home in England.

To buy clothes was another problem. We were allowed twelve coupons every three months to buy wools or cashmere, and naturally everything we wanted was wool or cashmere. Nylon stockings were out of the question. No one had any. We got them through friends or family who mailed them, one by one, in letters. My aunt often sent me food, too, and Julie's mother did the same. We invited our English friends over for dinner when we received boxes from home.

Most of the members of the company had found apartments, so we rotated our dinners on Sundays when we did not work.

The idea of having royalty in our audiences now and then sort of stimulated our interest. The word would scale the walls, settling backstage, when a royal personality was anywhere nearby. Every theater in London, of course, contains a royal box, so it was natural for our eyes to glance there first on entering the stage. We were terribly disappointed when kings and queens did not look down on us.

The night that royalty did come in, there was a great discussion, involving Miss Dunham particularly, as to whether she should bow, curtsy, lower her head, or forget the whole thing. There was still a dispute as to what the American should do under the circumstances. Then, too, if Miss Dunham acknowledged the presence of royalty, what should the cast do?

We were in our places on stage, watching Miss Dunham's entrance with careful eyes, waiting for her to offer an American greeting to British royalty. On her cue, she came on the stage, almost facing the royal box. She nodded her head in rhythm with the drums, without disturbing the choreography. If one did not know, one would have thought it a part of the dance.

When time came for me to do my little number with Jessie Hawkins, I fixed my hair the way Miss Dunham always told me not to, because I wanted to be more attractive. Since I was singing a Spanish song, I could not understand why she made me wear a bandanna over my hair. She would watch from the wings when one least suspected, to see if her orders were being carried out. They were not this night, for I fluffed my hair in bangs, with curls all over my head, and pinned the bandanna on a small portion of my hair with the hope that it would fall off at some interval. I was prepared to take the punishment afterwards and went offstage prepared for the worst.

Since I had got away with that, I figured I could take another chance in the finale of the first act, a number called "Shango." This involved the sacrificing of a white cock to the god of Shango. We all got possessed, and one boy turned into a snake and slithered all over the stage. I stood on the shoulders of two boys, dove to the floor, and slid from one end of the stage to the other. It was murder on my breasts, for we were not allowed to wear bras. Anyway, in this jungle ritual, just as the boy was being prepared to become a snake, I, as a high priestess or something, grabbed a cowbell and, running across stage, started a chant.

The chorus answered. In a high shrill voice, I repeated the chant with variations, leaping to a table, where I stayed, doing various movements and shouting until the curtain descended. When the curtain did come down, I was near death. It is almost impossible to sing with any meaning and dance with any meaning at the same time. Also I was afraid to do too much movement on such a high level, for Miss Dunham always restricted us from expressing ourselves too freely in the dance. Then too she did not want her choreography distorted in the slightest manner. If she had seen what I saw from some of us, when she was not looking, she would have been shocked into her grave long ago. Dancing on a table was not easy either. Very often I had to jump off when it toppled over and, with this particular in mind, I could never concentrate on more than one thing, singing, dancing, playing the cowbell, or keeping the rhythm.

Another fetish of Miss Dunham's was our make-up. Very often we would want to emphasize certain features—mine were my eyes and my high cheekbones. But Miss Dunham would say, "Kitty, you have too much make-up around your eyes." Or, "Too much rouge . . . cover up your hair." From the front of the house we thought all the girls looked alike and all the boys looked alike.

For six months, the Prince of Wales Theater was the center and the joy of the London theater district. Ours was the most exciting show that had hit London since the war. London still grieved from that horror—I could see and feel her wounds. I was glad that I was born in a part of the world that had been so well protected, but I was also ashamed of my protection. I carried guilt inside for being a privileged character when the rest of the world was being destroyed. My feelings made me realize how valuable my American passport was.

We were told never to let it out of our hands for any reason, no matter how well we knew the person who might ask to borrow it, for people all over the world paid fortunes for an American passport. I was offered money several times for my document. "You can say you lost it," I was told, but I would not let it out of my sight.

A few months before the end of our London engagement, I was introduced to a very handsome boy who took a fancy to me. I don't remember his name, but I do remember what he looked like. Along with the other girls, I thought that he was an extremely handsome son of a gun.

Since I had not yet got Charlie out of my system, I was not the warmest person in the world to him, but this did not keep him away. He met me at the stage door every night and drove me home in his little Jaguar. That is, when he was in London proper, for he lived on the outskirts of town. He spent Sundays with Julie and me, eating dinner and sitting around the fireplace telling stories. Sometimes he brought a friend, sometimes some of the company spent the day with us. In the evenings, we would go to the movies, for a ride in the car, or just walk, for London is rather dead on Sunday.

I liked being with him because I thought he was a perfect gentleman. He never tried any fancy business with me. I was hoping he would stay like this. For the duration of the time we were in London, he never made a false move, which I was more than happy about.

Anyone who even looked at me before then I practically growled at, because I had no desire for any man. It was a year and a half before I was cured.

I knew that I could learn to care very much for this boy, but, as it was, if he tried to touch me I would immediately turn against him. I did not like myself for being this way, but this was my mind's way of protecting me from another hurt. The day we left London to tour the provinces, he told me to write to him often, which I did once a week. I received a letter from him twice a week.

When London learned we were finally leaving, everyone came around with sorrow in his eyes, for we had made many friends. Many said London would never be the same without us.

We were not going to forget London either—I recalled things like the man in a raincoat with umbrella and a derby hat who stopped me one afternoon a few blocks from Piccadilly Circus, saying, "I say—aren't you Eartha Kitt?" He pointed his umbrella at me. I was so startled that someone recognized me, not only that but knew my name, I stood there grinning like a Cheshire cat, wondering what other miracle was coming. I said "Yes," and he took the carnation out of his raincoat lapel and handed it to me.

"I must pay you a tribute," he said. "I love your singing." He grinned, looking me up and down. I think he was more surprised that I was me than I was that he recognized me. "The way you move around on stage," he said, "is fantastic, but you are smaller than I thought you were."

I didn't know whether I should say thank you or just stand there and grin, wallowing in the praise. When I started to walk away, he grabbed my arm and said excitedly, "You must come and have lunch with me. I assure you I'm harmless and this is a great privilege for me." He saw my fear. "You need not worry, my dear. Here is my card of business. Everyone in London knows me around here, so you are certainly safe. We can go to a restaurant where they know me."

Since he wanted to go to a public eating place, I saw no harm in it. So I went, with a slight hesitation in my feet but, not my stomach, because I was hungry. In the restaurant, everyone did know him, or at least it looked that way to me. For the first time in ages, I had an expensive dinner. Anyway, here I was sitting across from this man who seemed all jittery at the idea of meeting me. I was still a little afraid, but I figured I'd eat the meal, he'd escort me to the theater, leave me at the door, and that would be the end of him. This is exactly what happened, except that he was waiting at the stage door every night when I came out, in the same raincoat, the same umbrella, the same derby hat, but a new carnation which he always presented to me faithfully. He would bow and depart in the shadows of the London streets. This went on until closing night.

I remember the time when Julie and I went to the Tower of London to see the old castle where the guards are dressed in thirteenth-century costumes, and when we walked across London Bridge. I had the feeling that any minute the bridge was going to topple. "London Bridge is falling down, falling down, falling down, London Bridge is falling down, my fair lady."

When we went through Jack the Ripper's playing grounds, I felt his presence everywhere. Any second he would dart out of a house and grab some damsel by the neck and rip. It was really weird if you went through there at night. When I saw Scotland Yard, I expected Sherlock Holmes and Dr. Watson to walk through the gates. We lived and breathed by Big Ben, the clock everyone looked up to. He never made a mistake. The British could always depend on him, and time was one thing the English seemed meticulous about. If you wanted to remain in their favor, you had to be on time. We had been warned about this on opening night. At eight on the stroke, the stage manager would take his knocker, which was new to us, and start pounding away on the floor just beside the stage so everyone in the building could hear it. This meant the play had begun.

Now we were leaving all this. We had been in London just long enough to want a change. It was a city that I never fell in love with but had grown fond of sanely.

Our first stop outside London was Liverpool, town of old slave markets, of flesh for gold. We were in Liverpool for a week, I think, maybe two. I only remember the uncomfortable feeling I had when I walked the streets. The loathing of the waterfront where the slave boats had docked—this was where it all began, with Africa directly across the sea. I used to stand on the pier for hours staring out over the water. Was I feeling sorry for them that are no more, or was it for me, a descendant of them?

The hotel pension was comfortable. I had a fireplace. With a shilling, you could get fire. For breakfast we had baked beans on toast, with a piece of tomato, or broiled kippers with dry toast and tea. No cream and one lump of sugar. I was more than happy to leave Liverpool.

Birmingham was the cold place. We stayed at private homes, and here we felt the blood of England. When we arrived at the house, Julie and I, there was the tiniest fire burning I ever saw. The lady of the house sat us down and gave us some hot tea to warm us up. She was a warm personality, which I could not understand, because to me this was the coldest house I had ever been in. When we were taken upstairs to our rooms, I was convinced of it.

A large double bed made sleeping more than comfortable for us. At least Julie and I had no trouble keeping out of each other's way during the night. A basin and a pitcher of cold water on the table in a comer for washing purposes.

The bathroom was down the stairs, around the bend and out of sight.

Since no one in all of England had any coal, we could not expect any more than one piece of coal to be burning at a time. For two weeks, I didn't take my pajamas off until I had to go on stage. I wore fleeced boots that went halfway up my legs; my pajamas were also made of fleece wool. I wore several long-sleeved sweaters and was glad to wear bandannas to keep my head warm.

This was the time Roxie flooded the theater and we almost didn't go on. We all had our little company chores to do to prepare the wardrobe. Some things had to be cleaned, some had to be mended. Roxie's job was to iron. She was on the third floor; dressing rooms were on the second floor. Naturally the stage is on the first. Roxie leaned the hot iron next to a sprinkler pipe, the sprinkler pipe went about its duty and warned all the other pipes. Within five minutes, one side of the theater was flooded, costumes and all. So many fire engines turned out you would have thought all of Birmingham was burning down. Although half the stage was wet, the catastrophe was all backstage. The audience never knew what we went through trying to save our costumes in order to show off in front of them. Except for the cold, Birmingham was fine.

Manchester was the most pleasant. We all lived in a nice little hotel like a convent, quiet, with birds waking us up every morning. The hotel had gardens and trees all around it, which made me very happy. My room was beautiful, with an old-fashioned bed. High with posts. The bedspread was knitted figurines. The room was large and there was a fireplace. All I needed to start a fire in it was a shilling, which of course I never had. Our engagement in Manchester ended peacefully, for we did not get a chance to get too well acquainted. We hopped our little train to return to London, where we were to change for Paris.

Since we had a half a day in London, I called my little English beau on the outskirts of town. "Come and spend the day with us," he said. "I want you to meet my mother and dad."

When I arrived at the station, he was there to meet me. His mother was a warm person. I felt very comfortable with her, though a little restrained. What did she really think of me? Does she think I am a toy for her son? Would she feel better if she knew I was a good girl? I tried to read her mind, to feel her out, to communicate with her. She gave me no lead one way or the other. She accepted me cordially, but I suppose I was looking for more.

He glanced at me now and then with something in his eyes that I thought I knew, but could not put my finger on. Maybe I was afraid to. He was so gentlemanly, so understanding, so . . . for me. But there was something that carried from him to me, a warning. Somewhere along the line he was going to drop his poise and I was not going to be surprised when he did. I fought the idea of him disappointing me. Besides, how sensitive can one be when it comes to choosing men?

Later my sensitivity proved itself right. The place to tell people's truths is Paris. My angelic English gentleman came over to see me at the Paris Theatre. As I sat in my dressing room putting my face in order, a voice resounded through the walls, echoing the name which fitted the likeness of me. I trembled in my ballerina panties in fright. Surely the madame had heard, it being five before curtain. I spurted to my door to hush him before he could do any more harm. He came into my room with glitter in his eyes. The quiet one (on English soil) took me in his arms, squeezed me tight, and said, "Baby, are we going to have fun tonight!"

The curtain was about to go up, so I had to convince him that to see the show was the thing to do. He left in anxiety. Maybe I am thinking too far ahead of myself, I thought. Paris is too drastic a change for him. Maybe he's been drinking. I had been told about those flights from London. Air France serves champagne, and you can also have any number of those little bottles of whiskies. One who drinks doesn't know what country he is in, if he takes advantage of the hospitality.

I would figure him out later. I went on stage to dance my extra best. When the curtain went down, there he was. Knock, knock, went my door, as I took off my garments. Jackie and I started to giggle as we looked at each other, knowing what was about to happen.

"Who is it?" I yelled.

"Mel" went the familiar voice. "Let me in."

"Just a moment, we are not dressed."

"That's why I want to come in. Ha, ha, ha!"

I was so disappointed I could have cried. He was jovial, which I did not mind too much, but it was like turning over a card and finding a joker. He was so chivalrous in London. He waited outside the door until I was ready. When he saw me, he looked at me with, "Darling, I thought you'd never come out."

Laughing, he took me by the arm and proceeded to walk me through the streets of Paris. After the theater, I usually went with Jackie and others for food before going to my little hotel. That was my intention this night until he asked, "Where are we going?"

"Aren't you hungry?" I asked. "I thought we'd go with the others for supper. There's a wonderful restaurant up the street. We always go to it. Would you like to?"

"No, I'm not hungry. I'm not interested in food. I just want to go home."

"Home," I thought. We walked in the direction of my hotel. "I couldn't get you a room here," I said. "There are no vacancies."

He stopped and eyed me. "Why don't I stay with you?" I looked at him with disappointment but not surprise. "Come on," he said. "I hope everyone in the hotel is a sound sleeper, because we're going to have the time of our lives. Ha, ha, ha, ha!" I loathed him and all men at that moment.

I fought to calmness. "You can't stay with me," I said. I walked away, leaving him in the middle of the tiny Paris street, holding his overnight bag in one hand, in the other a cigarette trailing smoke in the cold Parisian air—to be swallowed up by that unvirtuous lady, Paris.

2

Paris was a fascination to me. The first night, in a cab on our way to the little hotel Julie's mother had told us about, Julie said, "Can you imagine, Kitty? Here we are in Paris. Isn't it exciting?"

I looked calmly out of the cab window. "I see no reason to get so excited. I knew I was coming."

The little hotel was attractive but far from swanky. We registered, writing our names in the space large enough for it and the other information anywhere on the card. Not knowing French, we guessed about everything. The only word I knew how to say in French was "no."

My room was fifteen feet by ten, with a basin in the corner. The bed was iron which reminded me of my childhood. The room rent was seven hundred francs a day, two dollars. We had told Othella and Jackie about the hotel and they soon arrived, taking a room together next door.

Our first move was to get dressed and explore the town. It was nearing darkness when we all met downstairs. "We should find some place to eat. I'm hungry," said Othella.

"Which direction shall we go?"

We followed the lights. As we passed various eating places, we decided not to try them. One looked too expensive, one had too many men in it. Finally, when we got tired, Jackie said, "If we don't go in here, I'm going back to the hotel and eat the mattress from my bed."

Just as we started in, a tall man followed by a taller one walked out of the restaurant. They looked us over. "This is the place I'd recommend, girls. The food's good," the first one said.

"An American," we yelled. The girls made such a fuss over him he joined us in our first Parisian supper, accentuating it with champagne. Champagne, something I had barely seen. Champagne in Paris. This I was not going to refuse. Drink or not, tonight I was the devil's child. Between the four of us, we emptied two bottles.

At the end of the first I could hardly see. I sat as still as I could, one eye closing after the other. We all seemed to be laughing over nothing—first one little giggle, a snicker, then a real hearty laugh.

Is this gay Paris? Each sip of champagne brought to my mind the warnings of my aunt. "You'll turn out to be no good."

"What's the matter, Kitty?" Julie cried. "Come on, have fun."

With guilt I picked up my glass every time they did. Glug! Glug! Glug! When the food came, I didn't remember what I had ordered and didn't care. When I realized how normal everyone else seemed and looked and how fast I was going under, I was worried. I must pull myself together, I thought. I might pass out or something. I have always heard the best thing to do is eat. I stopped devouring champagne and ate heartily.

After a while my eyes focused, making my surroundings clearer. We all ate, laughed, drank, smoked, joked, and laughed some more, finding out about each other. In the process of getting acquainted Julie asked the taller man if that was a gun she saw imprinting his coat. He grinned at her.

"A gun?" Othella screamed. The two men laughed. Julie pulled open the top of the man's jacket. Under the shoulder lining lay a small pistol in a leather holster. We all gasped.

"Don't get excited, girls. We don't waste precious bullets on girls like you," the smaller one said. That eased us a bit, but why? "A man needs protection sometimes," he added. "He's my bodyguard. Has been for two years." The bodyguard didn't talk much. When he did, I got the impression he was right out of the movies.

"Protection from what?" the questions started. "What are you doing in Paris?" "What kind of business are you in?"

He called for the bill. As he paid it, he answered our questions. I don't know how true the answers were, but they excited us enough. "I am the only survivor of a gang that operated in America."

"What gang?"

"The Purple Gang of Chicago," he said softly, with pride and ease.

We all froze a little. None of us believed him, but we could not forget the gun. It was just like us to fall in with gangsters our first night in Paris.

Anyway, they were Americans, so we felt safe. They drove us to our little hotel. They both said good night politely, saying they would call us the following day.

I went to bed in a stupor. That stuff sure was potent. I woke up the next morning at the knocking on my door. When I opened it, with half-closed eyes, I was surprised by the huge pot of flowers the boy held in his arms. The card said: "Mel."

I unwrapped the pot to find a bottle of perfume tied to one of the branches. Overjoyed and terribly excited, I wanted to run to Julie's room and wake her and the others up, but it was only ten. I knew they would be furious. I held my excitement to myself until one o'clock, not being able to go back to sleep. While she and I were talking about the gifts and discussing the previous evening, my phone rang. It was an old-fashioned one, French. I had never seen one like it before, in or out of the movies. It was on the wall, like the Mexican phones, but looked and acted like something left over from Napoleon. The phone would ring, I would pick it up, but it would not stop ringing.

Mel was calling to ask if I had received his flowers and if we could have dinner together. I told him we would all meet after the rehearsal at the theater.

We found the Theatre de Paris about ten blocks from the hotel. This was convenient, for we could walk and save money. The blocks were short. After a few nights of walking, we found we had company once in a while. If there were four of us, we had little trouble, but with two of us—or one, it wasn't so good. Once in a while it took a long time to shake our followers. The first couple of times Julie and I were followed into the lobby of our hotel where we called the manager. When we were first seen at night, coming in from work or whatnot, the professional girls of the neighborhood were suspicious that we might be moving in on their territory. It seemed our hotel was in the middle of the street-walkers' section. We were doggoned if we were going to move. We expected to be in Paris only a couple of months anyway. Why bother? The ladies swarmed around our little abode like flies to chicken gravy. We were a little embarrassed at times, going in and out, because our hours were pretty much the same as theirs, but we got used to it, until the morning we were awakened at eight by pounding on the door.

My room was nearest the elevator. "Who is it?" I screamed.

"Open the door."

"What have I done?" I thought. Maybe the hotel's on fire. The hell with it. They have the wrong door. I started back to bed. Bang! bang! bang! "What do you want? Go away."

There were voices in the hallway. Maybe something is wrong. I'd better open the door. When I did, everyone else's door was opened too. No one was around but men. One walked heavily into my room, his eyes glancing here and there.

"Your passport?"

"My passport? What for?" I tried to make him understand. If only I knew how to speak this language, I'd tell him a thing or two for waking me up at such a ridiculous hour. Other voices were getting louder. I searched my room, one handbag, then another, one bureau drawer, then another. Where was my passport? Could I have lost it?

I ran to Julie's room. She too was looking for hers. Then we remembered. The company manager had taken all the passports. We got on the phone to call him and he came over within the hour to rescue us from our fate. Of course we went back to bed.

But a French newspaper carried a small item:

FOUR DUNHAM DANCERS SEIZED IN RAID

During our first day at the Paris theater, our rehearsal had been witnessed by photographers, of course. Since publicity is publicity, we cooperated with the photographers, who posed us in various positions. Our rehearsal clothing being rather scanty, not revealing but scanty, it was just what the cameramen wanted. We were posed this way and that.

The following day Miss Dunham came into the rehearsal with a newspaper. Opening the paper to a picture of us girls, she proceeded to reprimand us for not knowing about photographers and how to protect ourselves from vulgarity.

She showed us the newspaper picture of the Dunham girls in rehearsal. When we saw it, we became hysterical. All that one saw was legs, legs, legs, no faces.

Opening night in Paris was fantastic. More silks, satins, sables, and lace than I had ever seen before. A stage was set up in the lobby. The decoration in the lobby was intended to create the atmosphere of a jungle. There was even a tiger peeking through the greenery. Animal skins and drums of all sizes and shapes, along with primitive art work, were displayed along the path to the theater.

As usual, just before the curtain was about to go up, something happened. I don't remember what it was this night, but word was sent to me to go into the lobby and sing a couple of songs to kill time until the proper show was ready. I was given a Haitian costume. That was bad enough, but to have to sing so close to people, as though at a party, was extremely difficult for me. With fear in my bones, I walked through the crowd to the temporary stage. I took the maracas and began my songs, not daring to look at anyone's face. Why one had to go through this kind of torture I could not understand, but I had my orders.

Finally the overture started and the ordeal was over. If we never danced before, we did that night for Paris. It was a wonder the Paris Theatre did not turn to charcoal when the curtain went down. Maybe it was because it was Paris—the beautiful woman with a controversial reputation. The one everyone wanted to make love to but few would accept for a bride.

For three months we went to bed at dawn. It was inevitable that I was awakened practically every morning by a bottle of perfume, champagne, flowers, or just a date for lunch. I got so tired I hated Paris and everything she stood for. I was too worn out to care. Of course I could have refused a lot of dates and hospitality, but I didn't want to miss anything.

3

The day we all took a chartered plane to Cannes was strenuous. We had to be at the airport at seven, after going to bed at one. Six o'clock in the morning in Paris is like six in the morning anywhere, except more so. I was so sleepy I couldn't get my eyes open.

It was my first time on a plane and I was sure I was dreaming the whole thing. At first the new experience did not impress me. Then the engines started up. As soon as my seat belt was fastened, my forehead was pressed against the windowpane. I sat in the first seat, just behind the propeller. I wanted to see everything. When the propellers started one by one to twirl the air, my fear became more acute. The vibrations shocked me out of my wits. If I have to contend with this noise until we reach our destination, I'll be out of nerves. I thought.

I dosed my eyes, feeling the airplane rise into the air with my imagination, though it had not left the ground. When I saw we were finally gliding across the ground, I thought of all the horrible things I had done in life. It would be just like me to get on a plane for the first time and have it crash. When the machine left the ground, I calmed down. I had never felt such serenity as I did when we glided through soft puff-puffy-puffs of puff.

I watched every cloud, every bit of sky, every object that passed my window, hoping to see an angel riding by. I thought this might be the closest I ever would get to heaven. so I'd better take advantage of it. Everything seemed natural to me after a while, though it felt very strange to be eating a meal hanging in the heavens.

Naturally we arrived safely in Cannes where the festival we were to be a part of was held. Cannes was romantic. The palm trees, the architecture of the buildings, the blue waters of the Mediterranean, made me feel the spirit. We did not see much of it. We walked around until rehearsal time, did the show, got on a plane, and returned to Paris.

I don't remember how long our engagement lasted at the Theatre de Paris, but it was terribly long. I was so sick of the place I felt as though I had eaten too much dessert.

Then one day a very handsome young boy came around. I don't remember how we met. Suddenly he was there. When finally we closed to go on tour, Philippe went with us.

Our first stop was Belgium. Brussels was an expensive venture for us. Since everything in the stores was American, American prices prevailed. We were told that the city was a little Paris and a miniature New York. This was no lie, because everything was American, including the taxis. We were grateful to be able to walk into a grocery and see U.S. products staring at us from the shelves. We bought up everything we could afford.

After one experience in a restaurant, we all decided to stock up on milk and milk products, bread, jam and butter, along with plenty of fruit. We used to eat in a cheap place next to the theater, our one hot meal a day. The hamburgers were great. That was our main dish, with a bowl of onion soup.

We enjoyed this city, even so. No one bothered us, only stared from a distance. Now and then a Watusi would walk by gracefully. Then it was our turn to stop and stare.

At the movies we had seen pictures of the tall Watusi. They fascinated me. Not only were they considered the most beautiful people in the world, but of all the African tribes they were considered the most intelligent. They were held in great respect, and their tribe was also feared. They knew how to bargain and how to keep from being exploited. One of the Belgian airline advertisements was the head of a Watusi with long lines in his face and high cheekbones. The eyes were wide and sensitive. These were one people I wanted to get closer to.

One day as I walked through the park, I had no idea I would come as close to my desire as I did. I stand five feet three, shoeless, which I was always proud of because I considered myself just right for a woman. I was never made so conscious of my petiteness as that day in the Brussels zoo.

As I stood there watching the lions, a shadow fell over me, something strange. When I turned, I saw the figure of a man that struck me dumb. My eyes glided up to see what the face looked like. This long, handsome face looked down on mine with a Mona Lisa expression that fell into completeness when he saw how surprised I was. He was surrounded by men a few inches shorter, his bodyguards, for he was a prince and was in Brussels on a tour. He stood seven feet tall.

When we went to Antwerp, I loved it, the old buildings and canals. The most impressive thing was the monument in the main square. Then there was the old castle on the water front. We were told there was a tunnel under it leading to Flanders Field on the other side of the lake.

Italy was next. Living in this country was cheap. There were so many lire to the dollar that large handbags came in handy. We could eat without remorse. Naturally, one's main meal consisted of spaghetti with various sauces, salad, and ice cream. I believe we ate nothing but ice cream the first two days because it was so different—tutti-frutti, spumoni, tortoni.

We were in Rome one month. This gave me a chance to walk at length through the streets. My soul reached up when I sat in the ruins of the Colosseum, and a visit to the city of the dead was a spine-tingling experience. The catacombs held my interest from the moment I descended beneath solid soil until I breathed fresh air again.

The people themselves were very friendly and curious. A group of people followed us for blocks the first few days trying to figure out what the devil we were. They soon found out from their newspapers and word of mouth. Our show was quite a shock for them.

Milan, Torino, Napoli. Poverty struck us in the face like a black cat leaping from a garbage can on a dreary night. Wherever we walked, children followed. Rags hung from their bony limbs as though God had forgotten them. Dirt sapped the color from their faces and hands. Their eyes glistened with expectations of a lira. Disappointed heads hung in fumbling hands when they did not capture a coin. Giving is a wonderful experience, but when it is endless?

When we left Italy, we went to Switzerland. Zurich was a city in a valley of high mountains. We were taken to a hotel pension. The beds were covered with a soft quilt of eiderdown that melts over the body in sleep. The stairs creaked from so much use.

We liked everything we saw in Switzerland. The quaint streets, the grand boulevards, the toy shops, the watch and clock shops, the lake running through the city, the high mountains, the snow peaks, the people—clean-shaven unless aged—no sign of poverty, the calmness, the serenity, the faces that continued to smile from one to another, the price of a heritage that made their eyes sparkle.

After a few days we got acquainted with people, those who came backstage after the show and invited us to their homes. One of them was a young man named Peter who went out of his way to be introduced to "the girl on the right." Othella, we thought. When we arrived at Peter's party, we were overwhelmed by the haughty group and by the huge living room with antique pieces encased in glass chests. Rembrandts, Gauguins, Monets, Manets, on the walls. The wide winding staircase.

Peter, who talked to Othella in a corner, looked up to find me alone beside the piano. He made his way to me and just leaned on the piano next to me. He said nothing, giving me the impression he wanted to talk, but had nothing to say. I felt his closeness and was sure he felt mine.

The cigarette smoke curled itself around the room and climbed to the ceiling, forming an invisible blanket over lonely souls. Everyone was impressed by Peter's world of luxury. Peter was impressed by our world and all of us wanted love. The uneasiness swelled into good-bys. I saw Peter the next night after the show in the restaurant we supped in. I had a haunted feeling for a while. My conversation became wild, my words had little meaning. I felt bored. I nibbled my food without appetite, wanting something interesting to happen to me. I sat with expressionless eyes one day when Philippe walked in the door. I had not seen him for some time.

How adorable Philippe was suddenly! He was more handsome than usual. I wondered if he was looking for me. He walked directly to my table with a gleam in his eyes, as though he was happy to find me. After the small talk, Philippe took me for a walk along the lake that ran through the city. He told me how he had longed to be with me, but that his father kept him so busy he could not find a way to get near. The words were mellow and sweet to my ears. I listened. Everything he said was what I wanted to hear.

He said he loved me. He said he was jealous to see me with other men. He wanted to spend every moment he could with me. The words were right. The hour of night. The odor in the air. The moon was in just the right place; the city was romantic with the fringed edge of mountains. The mood I was in could not have been better, but the mouth was wrong. I walked away from Philippe, ran-walked to my hotel a block or so away.

When I reached my hotel room, I wondered about Peter. Would he be a good man for me? But he likes Othella anyway, so I might as well give up. Maybe one day my prince will come. I covered myself with the comforting eiderdown that hugged me like a lover and I fell asleep.

Peter and I met again the next night at another party. He walked over and sat next to me on the divan. "You look sad," he said.

"That's my forte," I said.

"Meaning what?" he asked.

"To get attention," I answered.

"You've got it." We sat conscious of each other before he said, "I made a drastic mistake, you know."

"How?"

"I wanted to meet someone and was introduced to someone else."

Inside, my heart leaped, but I calmly said, "Really?"

"Really."

I wanted him to go on to explain what he meant, but he excused himself and went to another part of the room. I was left in a dither of wonderment, until he returned. I was dismayed because someone had taken the empty place next to me, leaving Peter to stand. I took a chance on him following me to the buffet table. He did.

When we found there was no place to sit, we chose the floor. He told me about the mountains and how valuable they were to the country. He told me of the food stacked away in caves. He told me of the dynamite that was also there. Just the pull of a lever could send the Germans and the city to kingdom come. He told me of the beauty of the mountains, the summer resorts, the health resorts, the luxury resorts, and the plain resorts.

"I'll take you in the mountains one day, if you like."

"I'd like."

Some people were leaving. "Well, I guess I'd best be going," I said.

"Do you have anyone taking you?"

"No—"

"Then I shall do so. That is, if you don't mind my little bug of a car." Among the rest we went into the streets. He took me by the arm and half ran across the street to what resembled a beetle. I crawled into it as he held open the door, having to stoop half his height to do so.

The beetle growled and spurted before darting out of its parking place. With a flash of speed, I was taken to my hotel door, at which we had to ring the bell. I dreaded coming home after one because the concierge locked the doors.

Peter said, "I know this old one. She can get nasty at times, so you'd better let me handle her." Which I did. I had no trouble this night, for the face of the concierge took on a new expression when she saw Peter, who left me at the door.

A few days later Peter took me to a resort up in the mountains. It took us two hours both ways. He called for me at ten in the morning, we hopped into his beetle, and we were off. The snow-capped mountains were thrilling. I felt minute and unimportant as we crawled along the feet of God.

The resort town was charming, with its tiny shops. The streets were bricked, the air was fresh and youthful. Peter took me to the ski quarters, where he prepared himself for a thrill. I walked through the snow with him to the cable car that he took to reach the starting point.

I played in the snow until he could be recognized flying like a birdman through the air, his skis splashing the angered snow to one side. My eyes watched in envy of the control of his body as it twisted and turned in perfect balance.

He gracefully came to a stop at my feet, saying, "Hi," splashing wet snow on my legs that were heated by the burning sun.

Peter removed the skis, took a deep breath and said, "Let's eat." We went atop a hotel and ate on a balcony overlooking the valley of ski jumpers, riders, climbers, and mountains. I ate the most wonderful food imaginable and made myself at home in the lap of heaven.

When we drove back to Zurich, the sun was setting. We stopped at Peter's favorite spot to watch the sun slide behind a mountain top. The moment it disappeared, Peter speeded up the beetle. Over a mountain and around the bend we saw the same sun set again and disappear.

We arrived back in time for the show. I did not go into detail about my eventful day to the kids because I thought it useless to describe. The value would have been lost in my small vocabulary.

Peter came every night thereafter to take me to dinner and home. I did not see him during the day because he worked much of it. Philippe began to take up my days with walks. I saw Zurich on foot and was glad, for I stopped in every shop I saw, aggravated because I could not afford to buy anything. Our successful engagement came to an end, much to our regret. Just when we were finding new friends, we had to travel on. Peter took me to the train and loaded me down with boxes of chocolate. He stood on the platform, waving good-by in forlorn spirit. I hung out of the window as far as I could, holding on till the last minute to a dream that might have come true. I had chocolate for a week, after giving each member of the company a box.

Our next stop was in Sweden, the city of Stockholm. We were put into a pension that was very nice. Miriam Burton and I had an apartment next to Othella and Jackie, sharing the same bath. We made ourselves very much at home in this part of the world, because the people were very friendly, very health conscious, and so clean it was frightening.

The city is built on little islands, which made it more interesting and unique. The shopping district was on one island, the sports and health centers were on another. The theater and amusement center was on one, the oldest parts of Stockholm were on another. All these were connected by little bridges.

The theater was a converted circus house. We were there for a month, not wanting to leave at the end of the engagement. The people seemed happier than anyone in the world. Every face and hand was immaculate. No torn clothing, no beggars, no drunkards. This was a perfect example of civilization. In amazement I went through the city without seeing one sign of a slum.

I could not get too close to these people, for friendly as they were, they kept very much to themselves in thought. The fact that there was never any drinking in a public place without eating kept drinking to a minimum. That is, until Saturday night. When you do catch a drunken Swede, he is really drunk.

I spent my days getting steam baths and massages and bicycling into the country with a boy I met who spent his weekends touring me around. The one thing that amazed me was the curiosity of the people. Not having the experience of seeing a Negro every day, they followed the darker members of the company around.

Although I lived a very healthy life there, I did not get much sleep because the evenings were so pleasant and the sun never went completely down. From about nine to twelve midnight, the night was a normal night. At one A.M. it was really A.M., for the sun was already creeping in. I was told that an hour or so away, in North Sweden, the sun never shone for six months and was never out of sight for the next six. I couldn't imagine myself living for half a year and sleeping for half a year.

4

From Sweden we went to Paris for a rest that we all needed. For ten days, we fiddled around our home grounds. No money, of course, but we managed.

One day when Philippe came to the house, I could not get up. When I tried, both legs gave way on me. As he caught me, I felt a sharp pain in my lower regions. I got frightened. He got me back to bed; then he went to call a doctor.

Philippe made an appointment for me to be examined. I was put in the hospital that afternoon at four. Nothing too serious. Too much fatigue, not eating correctly—no regular hours.

I came out of the hospital on Thursday; the company left for Holland on Saturday. After the long train ride I was in misery when we arrived in Amsterdam that evening. I did not sleep all night and decided to see a doctor next morning. The doctor told me I had to go back to a hospital for proper care. I went to the rehearsal Sunday evening and told them I was going into the hospital Monday morning. I had made up my mind not to let them talk. me out of it. I went into the hospital and remained there for ten days, looking out my window overlooking Amsterdam, with a lake below.

My amusement in the hospital was interpreting the Dutch that was spoken to me every day, since none of the nurses spoke another language. It was stimulating, because I had to think for the words, accompanied by signs, to make sense.

When time came for me to leave, the company had gone on. Someone was to come and pick me up, which never happened, so I took a train alone to join them. The company was delighted to see me and to see how thin I had gotten. The greatest concern of the Dunham company was gaining and losing weight.

By the time we returned to Paris, which was our next stop, I was back in form. We had a return engagement at the Theatre de Paris for six weeks. It was during our engagement there that Hugh Shannon, a friend of mine, took me to see Frede, the woman who owned Carroll's, a night club on Rue de Panthéon, a block off the Champs Elysées.

"She wants to see you," he said.

"Why?"

"Just come with me. She wants to talk to you. Maybe you'll be interested, maybe not. It's worth a try," he said.

We walked into an office that looked like a playroom in someone's apartment, with leather chairs and a soft settee. "Something exciting is going to happen; I feel it in my bones," I thought. At the same time I was scared. We waited for a short while before the tall, lean, dark-haired woman came into the room and took her place behind the desk, saying very formally in French that she was sorry to have kept us waiting.

Introductions followed. I was fascinated by the woman's beauty. Her hair was bobbed close to the skull, edged with a tinge of gray. Her tailored suit was a beauty. Her eyes were green and blue, with a slight speck of gray.

She sat fondling a pencil on the desk. "I saw your show," she said with a very deep accent. I grinned. "I wanted to ask you if you would be interested in working here for a while." I twisted my hands. "I don't know what arrangement you make wiz your company, but I thought I would talk to you anyway." I looked at my friend. "You don't have to give me an answer now. Sink it over." My friend looked at me.

"I have a Cuban singer, who is leaving in two weeks. I need someone to take her place. When I saw the show, I thought you would be perfect for zee job. I cannot encourage you, this is your decision, but one can never progress if he is not seen." I said nothing, leaning from one arm to the other in my chair. "You can double; there is time for you to come here and be on stage at twelve-thirty. Your curtain's at eleven."

I felt between heaven and hell. The idea that someone saw me and offered me personally a job—not through Miss Dunham but came directly to me. I had had offers of jobs before, but this was different. This was big time, not any two-by-four deal, but big time.

I walked into the theater that night in a big-time mood. Proud to be alive, proud of my dancing, proud of me. I told Jackie, my roommate, what happened. She was all agog. I put my make-up on in a hurry because I had to talk to Miss Dunham before curtain time. In make-up and costume, I knocked on Dunham's door.

"Come in!" I walked erect with nervous feet. I explained to her what my visit was about with, "I would like to double if I can, to see if I am capable of being on my own. I have no intention of leaving the company, Miss Dunham."

The prestige value would be infringed upon if members of the company were seen anywhere other than as a company, I was told. "However, I think you should speak with our representatives who are responsible for us being here. See what they have to say. They'll be here tonight, Kitty."

I thanked her and went onstage to warm up. I thought of the songs I'd sing—I knew very few. The dress I'd have to get. The music I did not have. I was afraid of what might happen to me if I took my life into my own hands.

I gradually gained confidence, remembering my sixteen hundred dollars in the Bank of America in Los Angeles. Anyway, nothing to do but try. How would I ever know if I didn't have guts to find out?

It was half a dozen in one hand of assurance, six in the other of fear. By the time the first act was over, fear had taken hold. I began to remember all the assets of being a member of the Dunham troupe. Prestige, the constant training to be professional, the freedom from having to go out in search of a job. I hated the thought of suddenly going out into a cold world.

As the curtain descended on the first act, I had made up my mind that if Dunham did not want me to take an outside job, okay, I'd string along as usual until something better happened.

I was called into the room adjoining Miss Dunham's to see our agent who represented us on our European tour, an affiliate of the William Morris Agency in New York. He talked to me in a gentlemanly manner about the obligation I had to them in the first place. In the second place, I was a valuable member of the company and, since our most exciting dancer had returned to America, they could not afford to lose me.

I was feeling pangs as he told me of the importance of being "loyal to the cause." He told me of the trials and tribulations of having to handle such a large company, that they had planned a tour of South America with all expenses paid. I felt ashamed of myself for being such a little heel as to think of deserting the ship when it needed me most.

The agent went on talking in a way that broke my heart. I felt so badly for my sins that tears rolled down my cheeks as I plucked my fingernails. "You should be grateful for the opportunity you've had, with complete protection." He raised his voice a little. "I brought you out here, I got you working permits, arranged all the tours. I am responsible for you." I felt him get tense. "If you dare accept a job in any part of this country other than with the company, you will not be able to obtain a working permit and I shall have you deported."

I raised my head slowly, looking him dead in the eye. I was hurt, deeply hurt, at this. I had not made a statement about accepting a job—I had asked for permission. I turned on my heel without a word, ran to my dressing room, wrote out a two weeks' notice, descended for my cue of the second act, and handed the closed envelope to an attendant, saying, "Please give this to Miss D."

In silence, I went on with the show. I felt my feet were sticking in clay. I thought of all the others who had left and wound up with no jobs, or married into a bored life, or come back on bended knee. But I would not be moved. When the final curtain descended, my whole body trembled with fear.

No one knew of my notice except those one or two. We were called back on stage, the usual procedure after almost every show. I sat on the sacrificial table that held me in the finale number, with my head hanging low as I heard the soft voice of Miss Dunham saying, "Rosalie, see if you can find someone to take Kitty's place. She has given in her notice."

A gasp went through the company. I felt all eyes on me—should I repent my sins and be forgiven? Jackie put her arm around me and we walked upstairs to our dressing room. The theater was not its usual noisy self. Many were meditating, some were rationalizing, others did not believe, some were glad. I felt the different moods in the walls and the air.

I left the theater a lost soul and lost myself in the walls of my hotel room. My friend came to call for me the following evening to find out what I had decided. We talked for an hour before we decided to put the whole situation in Frede's lap. What with this business of not getting working papers and being deported, I was pretty frightened.

"I don't believe that," my friend said. "Frede will know what to do."

We both went to Frede. "Don't worry about zat," was Frede's answer. "Besides, instead of opening in two weeks you can open when you like."

"I can't do that," I said. "I really don't have an act or anything to wear," I said.

"I will see that you have the proper rehearsals with the Cuban band. You and the leader can get together on ideas, he will help you. Sing the songs you know. Four or five should be enough," Frede went on." I will pay you ten thousand francs a night."

Ten thousand francs a night. I figured that was thirty-five dollars a night, seven nights a week brought it to two hundred and forty-five dollars a week. Quite a jump from ninety a week. Where will I be in a month, though? Frede gave me a guarantee of two months' work, which gave me another boost. Finally she advanced twenty-five thousand francs to pay for a dress and gave me the address of a couturier who was fast.

In three days I was ready, with a conglomeration of Afro-Cuban and Negro spirituals, ending with a little Cuban dance. The leader helped me a lot; he made all of the arrangements.

Opening night I ran into the club from the theater, very nervous and excited. Frede had advertised a little, so though I said nothing to the company, some of them knew. In my dressing room, Hugh Shannon, my friend who talked me into this, was as nervous as I was. Among the flowers of encouragement and luck, a bottle of champagne greeted me at the door as I entered, and my gown was laid out by some thoughtful acquaintance. My fingers were numb as I fingered my way into the white silk dress. It was strapless with a drape on one side, punctuated by a big pink rose.

I looked at myself in the mirror, thinking I looked innocent enough for a cabaret act. As I was about to go on stage, Frede came in, took one look at me, and declared, "Mon Dieu, where do you sink you are going like that?" Rip went my angelic dress up the left leg to the middle of the thigh. Before I could say Jack Robinson, I was pushed on stage as the music blared up and I was being announced. "Ladies and gentlemen, we present to you a new discovery, Miss Eartha Kitt."

My senses told me I was standing in front of people, that I should give a reason for my eccentric behavior, or excuse myself and leave. My only excuse was to sing, as I could see, so I opened my mouth and out came a sound called singing. The applause after each number was soul-satisfying, as it told me I was accepted.

At the end of my fifth song, I did a little pelvic movement of a dance, with a Cuban twist, the hip movements getting smaller and smaller. A shrug of the shoulder brought the end of my act and applause as the spotlight blacked out.

When I reached my dressing room, Frede came back to say how pleased she was and that I had a job for as long as I wanted. Since there is only one show a night in Carroll's for each artist, all my friends, including a few members of the company who surprised me by coming, went with me to the Café de Paris for breakfast to celebrate my happiness.

In Paris one has to depend largely on word-of-mouth publicity to be successful, and word-of-mouth seemingly was on my side. Frede helped me a lot with advertisements, too. She stood on the stairs every night like a mother hen watching to see that everything went smoothly. She treated me more or less like a daughter, and saw to it that I was not molested.

I moved into a little hotel in the Latin Quarter on the Left Bank. My room was much more comfortable than before and I made myself very much at home, since my stay was going to be indefinite. The door of the hotel was locked at one A.M. and was opened by a grumbling concierge who owned the place. It was like a family home, with everyone knowing everyone else. This is where I met

Bill, who lived on the top floor in a ten-by-eleven room. He kept warm with a burning candle and wore his pajamas under his pants. He was a typical Left Banker who ate in restaurants of the students. Bill was a skinny little Texan with a pleasant personality. He made me laugh more than once the way he pinched pennies. I was amazed at how far he could make a franc ride.

He would tell me jokes and dance around his room, showing me how subtle he was on his feet and telling me how he wanted to be in show business but could never get a decent break. He wanted to be a designer if he could not make the grade as entertainer. Poor little Texan, I thought, he has a lot of courage and ambition. It was not until I returned to America that I learned his father owned oil wells in Texas.

5

One night as I sat in the Café de Paris, laughing with some South American friends, chatting away in two languages, a young good-looking American walked over to my table and said, "Uh, excuse me, Miss Kitt, but are you going home any time soon?"

I looked into his face and started to laugh. "I beg your pardon?"

"Are you going home soon?"

I must have given him a questionable look in between the laughs, as I said, "What a hell of a way to be picked up."

He said, "Oh, I beg your pardon. I didn't mean to be rude, but I was sitting there at the bar, wondering how I was going to get home when I spotted you." We all looked at him inquisitively. "I was out with a party tonight and spent all my money. So I have no means of transportation. You live just a block from me, so I thought maybe you'd let me share your cab."

I was so fascinated by the nerve of this one that I invited him to sit down and join the party. He introduced himself as B. B. The party soon broke up and then I took Mr. B. B. to his hotel. When he reached it, he said, "If you will lend me a thousand francs, I can take you to breakfast. I will pay you back in a day or so."

"Why don't you just call it quits here and I won't owe you and you won't owe me?" I said.

"Because I don't want to leave."

"That's very nice, but it's way past my bedtime."

"You can't go to bed now, the sun's coming up."

I wasn't really interested in going to bed, but I wanted to see if he was a "I won't take no for an answer" one. He was, because he would not let the cab driver drive away. "If you won't lend me the money, why don't you take me to breakfast and I'll forget the whole thing?"

I was too tired to argue, and I loved the determination he had. The cab driver took us to the favorite all-night breakfast nook of show people. As we walked in the door, he was greeted from here and there by girls, girls, and a boy. Very popular, I thought. A few people whispered my name, to make me conscious of the fact that I was becoming popular in Paris. My engagement at the club was already two and a half months old. Paris was gradually becoming safe ground.

B. B. and I took a table in a corner and ordered. We did not talk too much because there was not too much to talk about between us. He told me how he had sat at the bar for a long time, making up his mind to confront me, hoping he would not be told off.

After breakfast, he walked me to my hotel, where I had to ring the bell to be let in. "I wish you wouldn't go up," he said.

"I must. These are not my kind of hours."

"Once in a while won't hurt." I waited patiently for the concierge. "Why don't we go swimming? You go upstairs and get your bathing suit. I know a wonderful place just outside of Paris."

"At this hour of the morning?"

"Sure, this is the best time." The concierge opened the door. I stepped inside. "Don't go up," I heard faintly behind me as I said good-by and ran up the stairs.

I was undressed and about to get into bed when I heard pebbles on my window. A whistle followed. It must have been him. More pebbles and silence. How romantic; just like the olden days. Hark! A lover beneath my window. Shall I be Juliet and look out? "Romeo, yonder stands my Romeo, three stories below."

I was amused and touched by this at eight in the morning. I went to the window to shoo him away.

"I won't go until you come down."

I decided to pay no attention to him. The pebbles kept flying. I began to get a little nervous, fearing he would wake up the hotel. I shushed him, got dressed, and ran down the stairs into what was to be one of the happiest complications of my life.

For ten days, we shared our time together. He took me to his duplex Montmartre apartment. He built a fire that we sat in front of the rest of the morning, talking, sipping coffee, dunking French bread. He took me to work every night, waited for me, we ate breakfast, and he would escort me home. We became very much attached to each other in ten days.

B. B. was warm and affectionate, remembering I was a woman at all times and treating me with just the right touch, the right words, and so much *savoir-faire*. His continental education had molded his American ideas. I found that an American with continental background is a man yet to be beaten.

One day, Eddie, one of the men from the agency office, came into the bar where I met my friends every afternoon, looking for me. I was laughing at the jokes the boys were telling me when he walked in the door.

"Kitty," he said softly, as he stood over my chair, "we just got a phone call from America from someone by the name of Wayde. They said you should call as soon as possible, that your aunt is ill."

I felt a quiver inside. My aunt had wanted me to come home for a long time. I had been promising her I would because every week it seemed the Dunham troupe was on the way home. In her letters she had indicated she was going to have an operation for a tumor of some kind, but she never hinted that it was serious. "I'll try and wait until you come home," she said.

I felt very close to my aunt the last year or so in Europe. I had told me of her neglect of me and how I had felt the need of love. She in turn wanted me to come home to be with her. We had talked of getting a larger apartment in a better neighborhood and of living a bit more decently than before.

"Why should they be calling me, though?" I thought. I had had very little to do with the family for years. I had lost contact with them. That night I put in a call to the Waydes. For three days I could not get through. When I finally did, Bernice talked. "Where have you been?" she asked. "We have been trying to reach you for days." She went on.

I broke in to ask, "How is my mother?"

"She kept asking for you," she said. "Why didn't you come home?" Then she added, "Darling, your mother's been dead since Wednesday."

Mumblers mumbled with the tinkling of Hugh's piano faintly in my ear, as I tried to make sense of what my ears had heard. "Wednesday," I thought. Today is Tuesday. Why didn't they tell me she was ill? Why didn't I go home when she asked me to? I held the phone away from my ear, Hating man for inventing it. Hating the distance between me and there. Should I go home now, to nothing, to a world I wanted so much, that's left me empty of all my hopes?

The tinkling of the piano with laughter from the bar seeped into the telephone booth, making me conscious of a present world, the world that momentarily I did not want any part of. I wanted to live my last two years over again so I could go home to find my aunt wanting me without regret.

The voice on the other end became alive. "Baby Girl, Baby Girl, are you all right?"

"Yes, I'm all right."

"We'll get money from the insurance people and send you a ticket to come home."

I said good-by and returned to my table. The word went through the bar like fire. The music and chatter continued with an air of false gaiety. Drinks were suddenly crowding our table in an effort to make me drown my sorrow.

Some days later I received my one-way ticket to home. The morning I was to leave, my friends gathered at my hotel at ten in the morning to take me to Gare des Invalides. On the way we stopped at a girlfriend's house. She had champagne ready to be soaked up in farewell. I was given a giant-sized champagne glass that held half a bottle. We made a loving cup of it. I gulped it down like orange juice because I did not want them to think I was too much of a sissy. Then, too, all this was for me, so I had to show my appreciation.

One glass went around the room in a chugalug fashion. Fast and strong. Another glass went around the room fast and strong. Another went around slow and weak—just barely making it back to me, who by this time could only see out of one eye.

I pulled myself together eighty times in that hour. One had to say adieu. We all went to Gare des Invalides in the little French cars. No one knew how splotched I was, for I held myself erect and correct all the way. Someone got the baggage set while the rest of us went to the bar downstairs.

"Let's all have a farewell drink to the one we love the best," someone yelled. When the drinks were set up, I had blackberry brandy. "Here's to Kitty, long may she live." "Salud." "I'll meet you here the first of October. Don't forget." "Down the hatch!"

Down my hatch went the blackberry brandy, falling into my stomach pit like a lump of lead, knocking me for a loop.

By this time the bus was ready to leave. I gave my gate pass to the driver as I kissed everyone good-by, vaguely remembering who was who. In a bunch stood all my friends waving sadly and calling, "We love you." "We'll miss you." "We've had fun with you."

As the bus pulled away, my conscious went unconscious and my friends and Paris faded away. "Don't you get off here?" someone asked me. I looked out the window to see that I was supposed to get off here. The next scene was the baggage. Someone took my ticket to count the pieces of luggage. I sat down to wait for the call to board the plane. There were my suitcases in front of me. "One hatbox, one large valise, one duffel bag, and that one on the floor is mine. They're all there. . . ."

I woke up lying on a couch with a woman in white uniform putting a pill down my throat.

"What are you doing?" I asked. "My mother is dead," I screamed at her. "Leave me alone—I don't want to see her dead—my mother—I want my mother!" A nurse gave me a glass of water.

I walked to the plane between two porters as they held me in a walking position. They strapped me in my seat and left. Vaguely a voice said, "Watch her; she's not feeling well."

When I looked out the window, I thought it strange that St. Peter was not there to say greetings of some kind. When I awoke I thought we had arrived in New York because everyone was getting off. I could not imagine where in heaven we were when I looked out of the window to see nothing but white fuzz. Since I was not coherent in my thinking, I thought it would have been rather strange to stop off at heaven's gate to refuel.

I had to let the cold air hit me before I realized we had stopped in Newfoundland where the snow was head deep and the ice was two inches thick. I fell back into another world. I woke up as the plane circled La Guardia Field. New York, I had not seen it for over two years. Someone I'm sure will be here to meet me.

I walked into the lobby of the airport, where Bernice and Buster Wayde were waiting for me. We greeted each other. As my bags were collected, Bernice told me how my aunt had packed an overnight bag one day, paid all her bills, and gone off to the hospital in the Bronx. We got into the car and drove back to the same house we were kids in, with Mama Wayde greeting me in grief.

She went on to tell me how they decided the details of how Mother should be buried. Whether her dress should be this or that or she should have the service of Salem Methodist Church or if she should have it down South. Whether she should be embalmed by this undertaker or that undertaker. Whether they should try to find me or not try to find me.

I longed for her to stop this agonizing tale of death, but I was brought up to be polite to my elders. "She wanted you home so badly," she went on. I felt ill at ease thinking perhaps I was the one who had not cared enough. If I had come home, she might still be alive. I would have been with her. But it was too late now to repent

I wanted to ask the cause of death but did not want any details that were not necessary. "That hospital," Mama Wayde said. "They should have known better. She had a tumor in her stomach that should have been taken out years ago. She had high blood pressure too. Then when they examined her, they found she had a bad heart."

I listened.

"When they asked her if she wanted to have the operation right away or be built up first, she said, 'Right away' and signed her life away. They knew her heart wouldn't take it, but they operated anyway."

I listened.

"They say when anyone packs a suitcase to go into a hospital, they never come back. She must knowed she wasn't coming back, paying all her bills and everything; she even paid her hospital bill in advance."

"I know I will never see you again," my aunt had said to me.

Mama Wayde went into another part of the house. I got undressed and went to bed.

The next day I got in touch with a lawyer who was recommended to me by Mama Wayde. "He will do everything for you," she had said.

My so-called cousins, a boy and a girl, went with me to his office downtown. He asked me a lot of questions about my aunt and my past that I answered as best I could. My cousins answered what I could not. The lawyer told me not to worry about a thing. "I will take care of everything."

I learned that my aunt had left over ten thousand dollars in insurance policies, of which my cousins had borrowed about two thousand to get my aunt embalmed and treated properly until I could take over. When I went into the funeral home, I was presented with a bill of nineteen-hundred-some dollars.

I said nothing when I saw the figure, for I thought it sinful to argue over death money. She worked hard for it, she deserved it. I made arrangements to have the body taken South, to be buried as she requested in the grounds of St. Peter's Church where my mother and my grandparents were buried. A few days had to pass before I could carry out my wishes.

In the interim, Josh White, to whom I had written, telling him when I was to be home, called and told me he would be right up. He was delighted to see me after so many years.

"How are things going with you, Josh?"

"Fine."

We chitchatted for a while and he left.

6

According to plan, my cousins and I took Mother's body down South. I had very little to say on the train and less when we reached our destination. All of Orangeburg turned out to greet our arrival.

I recognized no one as I stood on the platform waiting for the coffin to descend. One or two came up, but I could not break through the spell that was over me. I did not want to seem unfriendly but they were strangers now who had grown up and forgotten calling me "yalla gal." The memory was haunting me. "Yalla gal, yalla gal, yalla gal." I could almost hear it in the background.

I stood alone on the platform, away from that awful world. I could never come back to it.

The coffin descended, a cold black soulless box. I watched the men take hold of it without concern. This was a naturel function for them. I watched the coffin being put in the hearse and driven away. My body was empty—my muscles were taut.

I finally managed to act a little human when I was told to get into a car to be taken to my aunt's sister's house. The car was something left over from the days of Uncle Remus. The conversation was very limited as we traveled across a bumpy road into the woods and out again across the cotton field, down a little narrow path and the bend over the creek and into open fields and to a shambly shack. The scene was so miserable it was funny.

A fire was burning in the hearth, warming a room with slats out of the floor and cracks in the wall. The windows were covered by old croaker sacks. There were two double beds of iron.

I did not see the other part of the house until the following morning when I decided to make myself useful and cook breakfast or something. It was a good thing we did not try to communicate with each other much before I went to bed, because when I finally tried to talk to them, no one understood what I said.

I walked into a kitchen as primitive as Daniel Boone's. The wood-burning stove stood strong and round. The pots were out of my playhouse. Water had to be gotten from the well. They stood around and stared when I exchanged my city clothes for a pair of overalls to chop wood.

My cousin drove up, surprised to find I had made myself at home. She pulled me aside and said, "You sure surprised me, girl. I came over to see if they were having a hard time with you. You sure are a good sport."

The next day was the funeral. That morning early I got up with my so-called aunt to go shopping. "I ain't got nothin' to wear to a burial," she had said. "The chillin ain't have nothin' too."

I outfitted the chillin and her for the burial. At the same time, I had all of them outfitted for school from head to toe, inside and out. I had the house supplied with canned foods for a month or so, plus one hundred and fifty dollars in cash.

"You is good," I kept hearing. "You jus' like your aunt."

The husband said, "She came down here once when the church was blowed down and built it up again. Yes, sir, that's what she done." He went on. "Nobody forgits her for that." I listened to the husband and wife discuss her character with pride, feeling that I was getting to know her better in death.

We all got dressed in solemnity, washing ourselves in a foot basin after heating the water on the stove. I dressed in a black suit I had brought from Paris. By the time we were ready, Josh had arrived. He had told me he would drive down in time for the funeral. I got into his big black Oldsmobile, and we drove to the funeral home.

I sat in the first row, looking at the opened coffin. A purple veil was thrown over her because of the long period between death and burial. The little church of St. Peter was crowded. The services started in a solemn manner.

"We are gathered together on this unhappy occasion," went the preacher, "with tears in our hearts. . . ."

"Uh huh!" went the people.

"To pray for a soul that has left us," said the preacher.

"Amen!" cried the people.

"She was a good soul."

"Amen!"

"She was a kind soul."

"Amen!"

"We *know* she's gone to heaven."

"Hallelujah! Amen!"

"Uh huh! Tha's right. Hallelujah!"

"She rebuilt this church!"

"Yeah, she did!"

"She built this pew."

"Yeah, she did!"

"She gave us a helpin' hand."

"A-a-a-men!"

I listened to all their praises with pride and sorrow weighing heavily. I didn't want to cry for I had shed too many tears when I was alone. I was ashamed of not being closer to her than I was. She had found her identification among these souls. They probably knew her better than I did. In her death this was what she wanted to come back to. To be buried here, to have them say prayers over her. She never lost contact with them and constantly let them know that she belonged. They were proud of this.

They were sincere in their sorrow. No more helping hand from the North. Who will rebuild our church when the storm knocks it down? Who will send us city clothes? Who will donate to our school?

By this time the preacher had reached the climax of his sermon. "St. Peter, open your golden gates and let in this lonely soul who asks for forgiveness and for her soul to get cleansed, to be a child of God!"

He shouted, "Wash her hands . . ."

"Uh huh!"

"Wash her feet . . ."

"Uh huh!"

"Wash her soul . . ."

"Uh huh!"

"Accept her in heaven . . ."

"Amen!"

"Take her by the hand . . ."

"Amen!"

"And lead the way . . ."

"Amen!"

"Glory, hallelujah!"

"Amen!" a song began.

"Amen!" they sang.

"Amen! Amen!"

The church hummed the hymn of amen softly as the cries of "Glory be to God" were heard among the mourners. As the humming died out, Josh got up from the back of the church to sing a spiritual in honor of the dead. When he got himself set next to the coffin, the church became quiet as a mouse at the sign of the guitar.

A sinful instrument. I felt the uneasiness seeping into my bones. The mood was killed. I wish Josh hadn't done that. But I could not insult him by asking him not to—and I could not explain to them that the instrument was not sinful.

Everyone looked into his lap for fear of dealing with the devil. Josh sang, but he was alone all the way. My heart went out to him, but I knew that my aunt would have understood. He wanted to do something to ease the way, and this was the only thing he knew.

"Take my hand and lead me on," Josh sang.

The last note of Josh's song was barely finished when the piano started up in a rinky-tink way—" What a friend we have in Jesus . . . ."

The coffin was rolled in front of me. Her face was lovely. Her body was still. Her soul was gone. My loneliness jagged my heart and pulled the tears forward. My last view of Mother.

They rolled the body down the aisle to the graveyard. That lonely graveyard without tombstones. The graves were bare except for a few flowers. Even the trees had become tired of supporting so many deaths. The tombstones that were there had sunken in protest.

I stood at the head of the opened ground that was to envelop my mother. The coffin was lowered on ropes. Slowly it sank into a black world of unknown mysteries. "No more! No morel" "Ashes to ashes and dust to dust. . . ." They sprinkled the earth over the black box.

"Don't cover her up!" I called. "Please don't cover her up. I'll never see her again. Please! Please! Please! Don't cover her up—" Josh and some others took me away from the grave and put me in the car.

Back in New York I moved into a friend's house downtown. After three months, my money had dwindled to a few hundred and I was ready to get away from it all. "I'm going back to Paris," I said.

"No, you can't do that. We are getting you a job," I was told.

The job was to be at the Blue Angel. After doing a performance for one night, if I was any good, I was to be given a contract. The night that was chosen for me was Saturday.

On Thursday I started to panic. I knew I could not go through with that kind of audition because I was not sure enough of myself. In Paris I had broken through the barrier between public and artist. I could not face the idea of not succeeding.

To save myself the embarrassment, I got a ticket on the S.S. *America* to return to my world of safety where I knew I was loved.

PART FOUR

1

WHEN I reached Paris, I went to the Hotel Gallia off the Champs Elysées where the rent was high for my pocket, but the place was suited to my taste. I settled in my single room and unpacked. Immediately I decided to go into action by calling friends to let them know I was back.

"Orson Welles has been looking all over for you," Jessie said on the other end of the French phone.

"Stop joking, Jessie. Why would he be looking for me? He only saw me a couple of times at Carroll's."

"You better call him if you want to find out."

I changed the subject, making arrangements to be picked up that evening for dinner with Jessie.

"So you are the little girl Orson's been searching for?" asked Inez, as we walked into Chez Inez. "You better get over to that theater before it's too late." Maybe he is looking for me, I thought.

"I told you so," Jessie said.

The next day Jessie made me go down to meet Mr. Welles.

"No more casting," the stage manager said.

"This is the girl Mr. Welles was looking for," Jessie said.

"Not anymore," the stage manager said. "No more casting. The part's been filled." He opened the doors for us to leave.

I walked into the square in front of the theater, dejected and embarrassed. "No more casting" haunted me as I walked away from the grandeur of a mythical work. Jessie walked silently beside me.

"Hey, Miss. Hey, Miss," someone was shouting. "Wait just a moment." We turned around to the door of a cab flying shut as a kind-faced gentleman with cane and derby ran toward us. Out of breath, he said, "What is your name?"

"This is the girl Mr. Welles was . . ."

Before Jessie could finish, he said, "I thought so. Your face is much too interesting for you not to be the girl Mr. Welles wanted."

I grinned.

"No more casting, I know, but I wish you would come when Mr. Welles is here, so we can be sure of our decision. Say tonight at eleven—we'll be atop the theater in the attic room." We thanked him humbly. He tipped his hat and departed.

Jessie and I were on pins and needles as we returned to my hotel. I did not put too much hope in anything. I knew the part was cast, but it might be worthwhile for the future. That night Jessie and I went nervously into the theater; word was sent in to Mr. Welles that we were outside.

A huge domineering-looking hombre giant-stepped his way toward me. I felt the electrifying waves of his personality hit me as he drew nearer. "Where have you been?" his voice boomed.

"In America," I said softly.

"I thought you were in Scandinavia somewhere. Someone told me you were not to be found." My mind began to wonder about my friends. "Anyway, here you are. I am too occupied at the moment, but I'd like you to come and read for me tomorrow night. Can you?"

"Yes, sir."

"At eleven-thirty right here."

"Yes, sir."

He took my hand to shake it good night, almost severing the nerve. Jessie and I were so happy we had a drink of *vin rosé* on our way home. We met some friends who noticed I was all aglow.

"What happened to you?" I was asked.

"Orson Welles wants me to read for him tomorrow night at eleven-thirty."

"Really! What for?"

"A new play he's doing called *Dr. Faust*."

"How did that come about?"

I explained.

I couldn't sleep waiting for the next day. When the time finally drew near for my meeting with His Majesty Orson Welles, I was beside myself with calmness. We stumbled into the darkened theater, down three steps, through a dim corridor, up three flights, around a corner, through a door, where sat the personality of enchantment alongside the kind gentleman who, I learned, was Mr. Hilton Edwards, owner and director of the Gate Theatre in Dublin. It was at the Gate Theatre that Orson cheated his way into a star role by saying, at the ripe old age of seventeen or something, that he was a great American vedette. He also lied, he said, that he was twenty-one. He never told me how he got to Dublin at that age.

Anyway, as I walked in, the two gentlemen greeted me. I was given a chair at a table to read the part of Girl Number Three, who starts out as a student and ends up as Helen of Troy and who becomes Mary when the curtain descends. Confusing, I know; that was Orson Welles.

As I began to read Mr. Edwards commenced to direct me. "Leave her alone!" came from the side of the room where Mr. Welles was standing.

"I couldn't think that God would create a man such as you," I read.

"That's fine."

I read a few more paragraphs, going from youth to age, when I heard, "All right. As far as I'm concerned, you've got the part." I was too happy to get excited, too surprised to act surprised. So I was as calm as a cucumber, though my heart sounded through my chest.

"Be here tomorrow at one for rehearsals. I'll have a script for you then," I was told. I went home in a daze, feeling that I was anyone but me. I wondered how big the part was and came to the conclusion that it could not be very big. "You become his wife at the end of the play," I kept hearing Mr. Edwards say.

"Girl Number Three is the important one," the voice kept saying.

"She has scenes with him alone," said Mr. Edwards.

"Orson Welles and me side by side, on the same stage. I won't believe until I see." The next day I was up at ten, waiting for one. I got out my cutest outfit and left my hotel at twelve to walk off my tenseness on the way to the theater, which was a good forty-five-minute stretch.

"Can you learn fast?" Mr. Welles asked when I got there, handing me a script. "We open Saturday." Today was Tuesday. Everyone recited his part as I read mine. The stage manager directed me as best he could.

After rehearsals, Mr. Welles and I, with one or two others, stayed to paint scenery or go over our lines alone. Sometimes we stayed on the stage until wee hours of the morning, repeating lines to each other.

"The word is world!" he would yell at me.

"I said world!" I'd answer.

"Speak as though you come from New York," he'd say.

"How does one from New York speak?"

"Not the way you speak," he'd answer.

"Why should I talk like anyone special?"

"Because you are."

"Yes, but I don't want you to be conscious of it."

"You win."

The rehearsal would go on for another fifteen minutes.

"Why can't you speak English? You know so many other languages you can't speak your own."

"What's wrong with my English?"

"It's too clear," he'd yell. "You don't sound as though you came from anywhere. Everyone sounds as though he's from somewhere, but you—? No."

"The only way I can learn properly, Mr. Welles, would be to make mistakes—and since you are here to teach me."

We got along well together, for I took his direction as he gave it. No confusion or misunderstanding when he explained something to me, except of course for my English.

I was quick and willing to learn from him. With a tremendous hunger for knowledge I hung on his every word and expression. The rest of the company had to be directed most of the time by Mr. Edwards, who understood Orson well. Such a strong character and personality as Orson's could not be taken with a grain of salt, for there was too much pepper to contend with. He could not tolerate ignorance of any kind. If one was not quick enough, Orson lost patience. The quicker one was to receive what Orson had to give, the better his creative powers were.

He was pleased with me. I believe. in many ways, for he did not direct me too much. He allowed me to utilize myself as I desired. When I made a wrong move, he explained to me the character I was portraying.

One day I asked him, "What kind of a woman am I?"

"All kinds."

"How old am I?"

"All ages."

"Well, what period of time am I supposed to be living in?"

"All periods."

I wondered why I was chosen to play this particular part. From a teenager to a no-age woman, all in an hour, that was pretty steep.

At dinnertime I was often taken with Mr. Edwards to eat at Orson's favorite restaurant. I was introduced to gastronomic delicacies and listened to extraordinary tales and conversations. I sat numbed by the environment and speechless at the speeches. I never wanted to talk, for the knowledge that I was picking up by keeping my mouth shut was too valuable to distort.

Some nights when we left the theater very late, Orson and I would walk along the Champs Elysées in silence. The sun would be coming up and Paris would unveil herself. Paris was warm and fresh in the early morning as we strolled along her majestic boulevard to my hotel in silence. He would take me to my door, ring the bell, and say, "*A demain.*"

Opening night came. We had been in the theater all day, getting the last-minute touches done. The curtain went up and the play commenced. The first half of the evening was a thing Mr. Welles had written titled *The Unthinking Lobster*, a satire on Hollywood, in which I thought he was very funny. No one else liked it. The second hour of the evening was Faust. After the intermission, up went the curtain on a dark stage.

From the audience came three girls, Number Three being me. One of my jobs was to sing the queer little theme song, which said, "Hungry little trouble, damned in a bubble, yearning to be, be or be free, all that you see is about me." Words by Orson Welles, music by Duke Ellington.

The curtain ascends on a dark stage, as I said. Three girls come out of the audience, dressed in slacks and shirt (mine was a sweater), walk on to the stage up a set of stairs leading from the orchestra. The three girls are discussing who is to play Helen of Troy in the school play. One girl is the studious type, another the working kind, and me, whatever my instincts say I do. The three girls walk onto the stage moving a flashlight about. It falls on a statue of Faust, Mr. Welles in the costume Goethe meant Faust to be in. The girls continue to chat about Faust's character as two of them go off stage leaving Girl Number Three sitting in a corner of the stage in a very dim light.

Mephistopheles comes in behind Faust and begins a discussion about who was Faust's favorite playmate. "I thought you chose Helen of Troy as the most beautiful woman in the world," asked Mephistopheles, who was Hilton Edwards.

With the mention of Helen, the light on me brightens. "Helen," Faust says softly. The lights get brighter as I look into the audience.

Faust reaches out to Girl Three, who has just turned into Helen of Troy. She looks at him, gets up, and walks across the stage, where she kneels beside him. He takes her in his arms and says, "Is this the face that launched a thousand ships? Helen, make me immortal with a kiss." With this he pulls me close and kisses me romantically as the curtain slowly descends on a black-out.

The audience stirred as a few seconds lapsed between Helen of Troy and Mary, the next character seen as the curtain goes up again. Mary was me, alias Girl Three, alias Helen of Troy. Orson came back as John, also in slacks and turtleneck sweater.

He and I had a very dramatic scene before the mob came to get him, and I sing "Hungry Little Trouble" for the third time.

The play ended with me leaving a box, supposedly containing an invention of his that ticked, on the side of the stage in a spotlight. It held the attention of the audience. As the curtain went down, the ticking got louder and louder.

We took about ten curtain calls but we wondered how we were going to make out with the drama critics. The next day in all the Paris papers were Orson and myself— "The most moving voice in the world." "Orson Welles discovers great talent." "Eartha Kitt great find for Paris. . . ." And so on.

I couldn't believe my eyes—pictures of Orson and me everywhere. I even won second place in a poll for talent for the year 1951.

Then came the fuss. During rehearsals, the people from Carroll's came to the theater a couple of times to ask if I would be interested in returning. I said I would, naturally, but had to wait until the play was on the way. They got very anxious one day and were thrown out of the theater by Orson, who said, "Get out of here and leave her alone—she'll open when I let her!" That was the end of them until one week after the play opened. Orson then gave me permission to double at Carroll's where I had become what is called in France a vedette. I was well on my way to being anything I wanted to be.

After the theater one night I went over to Carroll's with Jessie to get ready for my opening there. Frede and I settled for twenty-five thousand francs a night in a verbal agreement.

One night Josh White, who had reappeared on the scene, sat in the first row of the theater as I went into Orson's arms. I wondered how he felt, seeing the one he had found so hard to control being swallowed by a giant of a man. Orson was not himself this night. Either he was feeling his oats a little more than usual or he resented something I was responsible for. Orson sensed Josh, Josh eyed Orson, and I was in between.

"Helen, make me immortal with a kiss . . ." Orson's fangs sank into my bottom lip and drew blood, bringing me almost to tears. His arms held me in a death grip. I could not move or breathe for an uncomfortable length of time. He threw me to one side as he exited, and I walked into another scene. As I stood waiting for the entrance of Faust, now to be John, I dabbed my mouth and saw blood. The swelling started when I was about to sing.

How could such intelligence exercise such pettiness? I went on with the play as though everything was normal, but I wanted to cry because I was so disappointed. When the final curtain kissed the platform, I darted at the vast figure, pounding away on the chest that topped my head.

"Why did you bite me?" I asked.

"Oh, I was just in that mood."

I pounded again and kicked. He walked away like the giant in *Gulliver's Travels*, brushing me aside like lint from his jacket.

When Josh saw my mouth was bruised, as we sat at the sidewalk café a few minutes after curtain, he asked, "What happened to you?"

"I fell into a wall," I said very convincingly. But one of the kids spilled the beans.

"Orson bit her," I heard from behind us. One leap from the table took Josh on the run. He reached the theater, which was a block away, just as Orson got into his chauffeur-driven Citröen and drove up a one-way street, against the traffic. I stuck to my story, but Josh dared me to go near Orson's dressing room or for him to come near mine.

I missed the old yell of "Kitt, are you ready?" from Orson, but knowing Josh's temper, I thought I'd better lay low until the heat was off.

2

After a six-week run in Paris, we gathered our belongings for Germany. The show was cut down to Orson, Michael McLiammor, and myself in a production of Faust. I wrapped all three girls into one character and was content to be a woman beside two such strong personalities as these were. The show was retitled *An Evening with Orson Welles*, though some Germans retitled it *An Evening with Eartha Kitt*. We did a peanut concert, with the short *Faust* as the first half. In the second half Orson opened with his magic tricks, after which he introduced me with very strong adjectives that I was always afraid I would not be able to live up to. I sang for fifteen minutes, then disappeared as Orson entered on an opened curtain with a scene from *Richard III*.

We started in Frankfurt. We had to work under a tent covering what was at one time part of a theater. The stage creaked and our moods were constantly broken, but we lived through it. I never knew what mood Orson was in until the moment to kiss. If he was gentle, then I knew his day had gone well.

During our stay in Frankfurt we were taken to breakfast one morning to a lovely home forty-five minutes from the city. We were on our way to entertain soldiers at a camp nearby. The breakfast was a banquet of collard greens, corn bread, fried chicken, hominy grits, hot biscuits, cold turkey, bacon and eggs, chitterlings, blackeyed peas and rice, pork chops, potato salad, topped with sweet potato pie, mincemeat pie, pumpkin pie, apple pie, ice cream, chocolate custard, whipped cream, hot nuts, and champagne. The house had been taken over by Americans from the Germans. The couple who gave the feast were ex-Harlemites who had found a paradise of peace and plenty. Not knowing what to do with themselves now that the tables were turned, they went overboard with everything.

In Hamburg I began to be more curious about the German people, but I could never get close enough to delve deep. Whenever I visited with families, the subject was always on the light side. No one got serious enough to be informative. They were all very polite, gentlemanly, and formal. The one time I sensed a warmth was in the home of a couple, Mr. and Mrs. Weld. We met them to have dinner and to hear a song Mr. Weld was writing for me. In discussing the meaning of the words and how he felt about my work, Mr. Weld conveyed a feeling of romanticism which made me ask myself, Is it or is it not dead among the Germans?

The tour was always interesting because there was never a dull moment, particularly with Janet Wolfe around. One night she came on stage in the mob scene of *Faust* and, instead of saying, "He's a horrible man, your husband," said "He's a horrible ham, your husband." It was comedy thereafter for the rest of the evening. Having this kind of thing to contend with, Orson made faces at me whenever his back was to the audience. He was a fun man to work with because one never knew what he was going to say or do.

Munich was one of my favorite places. We stayed at a hotel which served the most delicious salad in the world, made with apples, grapes, lobster, and whatnot. My days there were taken up by newspaper people who took me out often to show me the city. I was taken to the square where the little dolls come out at eleven in the tower and dance around a clock. In the square was a store where I was taken to be outfitted in a typical peasant costume, including straw hat. For lunch I was taken to a beer hall, where Hitler used to give most of his speeches, to have beer, cold cuts, and pretzels. The stein of beer was so huge I needed both hands to lift it.

Berlin was where I saw German theater. It was explained to me that the greatest theater in the world at one time emanated from Berlin. The scenery was so intricate, the curtains were handwoven, the lights were so complex, and the acting was superb.

Since Berlin was the dividing line between East and West, we could see both sides of the fence. Signs were posted everywhere in several languages: "You are now in Russian territory." "Long live Stalin." "Here begins the true democracy." On the Russian side of the fence, little life was going on. There was one car pitting along as we drove through, containing Russian soldiers. I felt a world without a god. Even the devil was afraid to make an appearance. The streets were bare except for a stray person or two. It was a very strict life in the Russian Zone. If anyone was caught leaving for good, he was of course brought back in front of a rifle.

It was so easy too. All one had to do was to walk across the street, leaving all his belongings behind. I was told never to cross the border alone.

What did the Russians look like? I wanted to know. I found out when I visited a monument in honor of the Russian soldier, which is in the British sector and is guarded by Russians.

I walked up the twelve or so stairs from the sidewalk to look a tiny little Russian dead in the eye. He looked at me as though to say, "What in hell is this?" but held tight to the rifle crossing his body. He was not allowed to move. This was against regulations. If he was annoyed, a button level with his elbow could be pressed.

"He's no bigger than I am," I said to Orson.

I stared at him to see what made him tick. He became nervous and started to sweat. He looked as though he wanted to do something about me but was too curious. He was trying his darnedest to figure out who, what, and why I was. I looked down at his tiny feet, his knee-length boots shining my reflection. I felt sorry for him as I walked away, catching up with Orson who had gone to the back of the monument.

All in all, I loved Germany, including the bombed opera house and Hitler's scatterings. On my way back to Paris, I rode the Berlin

Express. It took great precautions against sabotage. All lights were put out at a certain hour. I felt very mysterious because of the atmosphere. Our passports were checked thoroughly and kept overnight. As long as my precious passport was out of my hands, I did not rest.

In a couple of days, I went along with Orson and the others to Belgium, where we stayed for ten days. Closing night in Brussels was not at all comfortable. Orson gave a farewell cocktail affair in his place. No one spoke to anyone. We just sat and looked at each other. At the door for good-by, Orson looked at me as though he wanted to say something but could not think of the word. At the moment he was ready to say whatever it was, Janet broke in with something smart that changed his attitude immediately and that was that. During the evening, Orson had said for me not to leave until he talked to me, but I left never knowing what it was he had to tell me.

When I returned to Paris in September I became terribly ill. My nerves, said the doctor, were in fantastic shape. I was in bed for three weeks without going out. When B. B. arrived on the third of October, two days later than he said he would, I was more than eager to see him.

"Can I take you to dinner?" he asked on the phone.

I did not want to refuse him because I wanted to be with him. "Come on over." I gave him the address and put my clothes on, hobbling around.

Three weeks I had lain there, hoping each day I would be better the next.

B. B. was more handsome than ever. He had been to Hawaii, and was back in Paris to live it up. We left finally to have dinner in one of our favorite spots. We sat beside each other in a tiny restaurant, wondering what was in store for us. He told me of his trip until we grew bored with sitting. We got reacquainted with one another, with Paris playing Cupid.

We walked for a while when we left the restaurant, in the glow of a moon that silhouetted the rooftops that said: "This is Paris." The wind was slight, rustling the leaves that hugged the gutter in memory of summer. We were still, with only the sound of our footsteps to contend with. I was happy for no particular reason except in the awareness of a new beginning.

I took to my bed again for some days thereafter, as I became much weaker. I was nursed day and night by B. B., who never left my bedside until I recovered a month or so later. All due to nerves, the doctor said.

I had word from Frede that a new club under her management was being opened in a couple of weeks. She asked me to reserve my services for the new spot. I was glad I was still wanted, for I had seen no sign of work for some time. No one knew I was in Paris, I was told. When I was finally up and about, I went to see Frede about the new club.

"The club is opening in a week or so," Frede said. I began to prepare my act and my clothes, anxious to get started, particularly since my hotel bill had been mounting for some time. When I had not heard from Frede the day before the club was due to open, I went to see her. "It will open in a week," she said. "We are having a little trouble."

I would return to my hotel every Thursday, waiting for the Friday when the club was to open. For one month I went back and forth, until I was exhausted. In my exhaustion my fury rose before I could control it—the suede coat I wore was flung to the floor as I demanded a week's pay to compensate me for waiting around.

"Don't accept another contract," Frede said. "We will open any day now."

"I won't wait any longer!" I screamed. "My expenses have gotten too high waiting for you."

I flung a chair to a corner of the barroom as I said, "You've made me wait three weeks without any money coming in. I must eat in order to be alive when your club opens. I demand one hundred thousand francs to pay my bills or I accept another contract."

"Oh, Kitty, Kitty, don't lose your temper. I will give you fifty thousand."

"One hundred thousand!" I screamed. "I could have been working by now. I don't believe that place will ever open. I won't leave until I get what I asked for." I stamped my foot and demanded my rights.

Frede disappeared for a half hour. When she returned she handed me an envelope containing one hundred thousand francs, which I counted before I stepped outside the door.

The following Friday the new Perroquet opened with a lot of ballyhoo. Every celebrity in town was there. The place was so packed no one could breathe. Since there was no means of ventilation this eventually killed the place after four months. After the new cabaret was unsuccessful, Frede asked me to return to Carroll's, which I did for a couple of weeks before accepting an offer in London. At the end of another three months I had offers from all over Europe, and one luring bid from Turkey.

My tour began in London at a club called Churchill's, where I was received with great enthusiasm and was made very happy by the thoughtful owner. The audience consisted frequently of royalty and important figures. I met many and made friends with quite a few. One was a maharajah who invited me to his establishment one night for late tea in the presence of a girl I knew vaguely, who accompanied us.

The long Rolls-Royce transported us from one end of London to another, where the aides of the maharajah knocked on a door that was opened by a turbaned Indian with beard and long nightgown. His feet were bare as he meekly welcomed us into the living room where a fire was burning.

All the aides disappeared as the girl and I made ourselves comfortable. One by one the aides returned, stripped of their uniforms and comfortable in leisurely gowns, turbans remaining on all. By this time the servant had brought in his slippers. There was Turkish coffee for all.

I sat in a soft chair, rearing back in comfort, thinking how close the world could be in a living room. The maharajah took a seat beside me and held my hand. I smiled at him, pulling my hand to me and extending it for a cup of coffee. An aide sat on the other side of me. He put his hand on my shoulder, running his fingers up and down the back of my neck. I hung onto my coffee, sipping to make it last longer. This should show disinterest, I thought. The more disinterested I became the more interested they became. The aide moved in on my left, the maharajah on the right.

I knew I shouldn't have accepted in the first place, but my curiosity got the best of me. I was afraid to put my cup down, but I did. My temples were being pressed softly. A feeling of sleep came over me. My arms were being massaged at the same time by the men at my side. Across from me the girl was being massaged by two of the aides.

I wondered what the intention was but I wouldn't let the carryings-on go any further. I got up suddenly, excusing myself to look at a painting on the wall. This led to my saying it was late and I should be home. The men were left looking at each other as I walked out the door. I got into the waiting chauffeured car and directed the driver to my hotel.

The night my engagement, which had lasted two months, came to an end, I took a plane to Paris. I planned to spend a few days there before continuing to Istanbul, Turkey.

3

When the agency had asked me if I would be interested in going so far afield as Turkey, I accepted gladly for I thought the opportunity might not come again.

"But no one hears of you in Istanbul," Eddie said. Meaning if you're good or bad, only the Turks will know.

"I don't care about that," I said. "My main interest is to go there." My contract was the equivalent of about five hundred dollars a week and expenses plus transportation.

"You must be careful too and get all your money in your own hands," said Eddie. If I came out penniless, I would not mind. I had grown accustomed to winding up with nothing, one way or another.

I said good-by to friends before taking the seventeen-hour trip to Istanbul. The world became stranger to me the farther East I went. The language became more tongue-twisting as the eyes narrowed and the cheekbones became more prominent, as the hair darkened and the skin became darker.

I got off the plane at a more or less modern airport, waving to wavers who waved at me. These must be my escorts. A very handsome dark man with a mustache flowered my arms with a bouquet of roses, while another took my baggage tickets. I was taken through customs to the sound of mysterious lingo. The dark handsome Jack spoke a little English. The other spoke French. Since I had nothing to declare in the way of import, my baggage was not opened.

A car transported us from the airport to the City of Seven Hills, along a long, winding, narrow, primitive road, passing natives in their ancient wear. Atop the hill where the gates to the entrance of the city stand, I stopped the car to see the view that lay below. The domes of mosques accentuated the picture. Continuing to the hotel, I watched the changes of architecture. Suddenly there before me lay the Bosphorus, the great gateway.

Fayard and Harold Nicholas stood in front of the hotel as we drove up. Gleefully I jumped out of the car, throwing my arms around both of them, for we had known each other for many years. To see such familiar faces in a faraway land is very refreshing.

I checked in and was shown to my room. The Nicholas brothers accompanied me to see that I was comfortable, giving me hints as to do's and don'ts. By the time I took a bath and dressed, the boys had to go to work, so I tagged along. Waiting for a cab on the sidewalk, Harold brought to my attention the fact that we were being watched by a group that had suddenly gathered.

"Funny, we never had that before," Fayard said. "Must be because you are a strange-looking woman." I took it that I should laugh at this remark, so I did. When we arrived at the Karavansary, where we all were to work, all heads turned as we walked through. A table in the balcony was reserved for the artists every evening, so I joined them.

The moment I could be seen from below, all eyes went up. I wondered all kinds of things about myself. Did they think I was beautiful, weird, exotic, mysterious, funny, or just another kind of woman? I found out on opening night, when I stepped on the little scene with feet of glass, expecting anything to happen.

As I stood at a pencil microphone, the room hushed to a dead silence. Something must be wrong. No group ever gets this quiet, I thought. What do they expect of me? I smiled, not knowing what else to do.

The music, being played by Turkish musicians, whose concept of American is only through imitation, started and I began a song. Halfway through, a soft whispering of the crowd mounted into a murmur. My feet of glass trembled, a choking leaped into my throat, my hands began to perspire. I felt more alone and unwanted than ever I could remember. There was nowhere to run so I stood in my place to try again.

My next song was a French one. The murmuring ceased when a voice was heard coming from the stage left in a Turkish tongue. I could not understand him. The room roared with laughter after each phrase of his that was heard, following each phrase of mine.

I looked toward the door in search of some consoling eye like that of the Nicholas brothers, but they were not there. The voice went on. The crowd roared. I went on.

When the last word was sung, I walked quietly and quickly off the stage, past the tables to the door that led to safety, where I was met by Mr. Kibor, the owner.

"You don't have to tell me. Give me my ticket back to Paris where I belong. I won't even ask to be paid, just my ticket."

"What are you talking about? They love you. They talked all through your songs. That was to show they were complimenting you. Can't you hear the applause? They want you back."

"But that horrible man . . . ?"

"He was telling them you could do no wrong, that you are beautiful, and he wishes he were fortunate enough to have you, to take care of you. Go back and finish your act."

By this time the compliments were over and I was able to go through the remaining part of my act in peace. When I went the rounds as I was asked to do by Kibor, I was introduced to practically everyone in the room. The people whom I met supported me for the two months I remained in Istanbul. I learned that, when they like someone, they become ardent supporters. To show my appreciation for being accepted so beautifully, I learned some Turkish songs, one of which was "Uska Dara."

After that, I could do no wrong. Kibor wanted me to stay for six months, but I grew weary of being so far away, though I had found many friends.

My Sundays were spent visiting the Dardanelles or someone's country home or just viewing the city. Aykut, whom I met through friends, escorted me about most of the time, taking me to the restaurants and museums. I loved eating in the seaside places and driving through the hills of the countryside.

During my stay in Istanbul I was told never to go out alone. I had always wondered why I had to be escorted to and fro all the time. Someone was on call for my every need. When Harold and Fayard were there, I was with them most of the time. When they left, I went to the airport with them in a cab. No one to bring me back. I had forgotten the orders—

On my way back to the hotel I went on a shopping spree alone. To my amazement, traffic was stopped, doorways were jammed, and confusion reigned when everyone stopped to take a look at me. When I tried to walk down the street I was mobbed by passersby who wanted to touch me, to get a closer look, to feel my clothes, to stroke my hair. The situation became impossible. Luckily a complete stranger took me by the arm and shoved his way through to get me into his car and away. I never saw the man again, for he left me on my doorstep without a word.

After being in Turkey for some time, peacefully minding my own business, I discovered through a mysterious letter that I was being sued by the Turkish government for illegal entry into the country. I had come in as a tourist and had obtained work, it seemed. This I knew nothing about. Why didn't someone tell me I was a tourist?

Off to court I went at nine in the morning with a lawyer. "Don't worry about a thing," he counseled me. "This is the regular procedure."

"You mean this is the way you get artists into the country?"

"The only way we can do it. They expect it. No matter what the judge says, say yes." This to me is a word that gets people into more trouble than saying no, but if yes was what he wanted, okay.

We waited for an hour or so before we were called, me half asleep. Some words went on between the lawyer and the judge for about fifteen minutes. Then silence. More words. The lawyer then took his coat and hat, helped me with mine, and took me home. "Meet you at eight-thirty in the morning," he said as he left me in my lobby. "The case isn't over yet." They'll put me on a Turkish chain gang and I'll never see America again. *Adieu, ma belle vie.* I slumped into my iron bed and escaped my misery.

The show went on as usual that evening, but the following morning found me again in the Turkish court. More conversation between lawyer and judge, who finally reprimanded me good and sent me home—after making me pay five dollars for being a bad girl—with a work permit.

I went to the opera one night with Aykut and his family. More faces watched me than the opera. I asked Aykut why so much attention was given me all the time. From the moment I entered the city I had been taken for an Egyptian princess, he told me. Kibor verified this later. As a matter of fact, Kibor said he had thought the same thing when he had seen me at Carroll's in Paris.

The women of the country I found very attractive, with spiritually lovely faces, but their bodies were a little on the stout side, particularly after their twenty-first year. I was told that they were all usually married by this age, and that every girl watched her figure until her man was caught. One of the things they found strange in me was that I was tiny in body. The girls were still chaperoned in most families, but not all. During the past twenty-five years a new regime had given them a bit of freedom and many were able to move about without guardians.

The men were dark and handsome, and four of the handsomest worked at the Karavansary. One of them was my escort. One day in a casual conversation he told me that he was a member of the secret police and that I had been followed for two weeks by his department because I was a friend of the son of the Admiral of the Navy. The question arose as to what my intentions were in going out with the son.

Whether his story was true or not, I was told every move the son and I had made on every date. Something else that made me realize how cautious the people are occurred the evening I was sitting at dinner with some members of the orchestra and the personnel. I mentioned an article I had read in *Newsweek* about Ataturk. The more I discussed the article, which explained the things he had done for the people and for the benefit of the country, the more silent everyone became. Within a few minutes I was sitting at the table alone. When I asked later why this happened I was told that no one discusses politics, good or bad, except in the privacy of his home.

When my contract was up and I was ready to leave, there was much to-do over a piece of paper about two inches long and two inches wide that would permit me to pass through the gates to another world. I learned that the difficulty arose because someone had tried to prevent my leaving. Kibor wanted me to stay for six months. When he asked me to remain, my answer was no, because I longed for Paris, though I had grown very fond of Turkey. It took about ten days to get the little slip of paper which should have been handed to me the moment I reported to the police department and asked for it. I was told that probably one of the admirers whose gifts I had returned had become annoyed and had tried to detain me in the country in order to make me change my mind. Diamonds may be a girl's best friend, but their beauty is only stone deep.

Besides, I never felt so far away from home as when I picked up the phone one day and said, "I want to make a long-distance call."

"Yes, where to, Miss?"

"New York."

"I am sorry, Miss, but you cannot call America from here."

I hung up the phone in a daze, trying to figure out just how far was I from home.

My plane landed in Athens, and I was met by Mr. Constantino, the owner of the club I was to work in, who calmly took me through customs. Again I was looked upon as strange, but not so extensively as in Turkey. Everyone smiled at me with love, but loneliness struck me when I heard an even stranger language than Turkish.

"Almost no one here speaks English," Mr. Constantino told me.

On the way to the Park Hotel, I saw the Acropolis standing high on a hill overlooking the city, veiled by the spirit of the gods who molded her walls with architectural love and left her a monument to themselves. Alone and crippled, pleading to be once again what she was, the home of thinkers, when all of Athens looked up to her. Now she looked down in hopes of catching a wandering eye.

My hotel was as modem as any hotel in America, with all the conveniences and luxuries. I made myself comfortable with a bath. Mr. Constantino met me shortly thereafter to introduce me to the club and the musicians. We got along very well, for they had mapped out a program for me which they thought would be suitable for their clientele—all the old American songs that everyone knew and loved. This turned out fine for the Americans who frequented the club. They were glad to have a reminder of home.

My opening was a joyous one. Mr. Constantino was happy, except for the hot weather, which is always a danger for clubs because people look for cooler places, but we stood up very well under it.

As for my days, I spent them visiting the places of interest. I took a closer look at the Acropolis. Her grounds were full of weeds. Poppies grew nonchalantly between her toes. Her remaining pillars stood straight and beautiful to the eye, though—or because—they were purposely crooked. There was not much to see, but it was worth the climb we did on foot to reach it.

The site, overlooking all of Athens, is hypnotizing and enchanting. I remained there for many hours, seeking a way to grasp the knowledge symbolized by these ruins of an ancient but never-forgotten world. My conscious hungered for all that had had to be to give me a taste of it, an essence to take with me. I never wanted to be old with knowledge but young with it. Spirits were here to haunt me but I had no means of communicating.

My stay in Athens for a month was a quiet one. Some of my days were spent with a Turkish belly dancer who tried to teach me her art but, alas, my stomach did not have enough of the elastic features that come from excess.

Mr. Constantino did not pay me my complete salary weekly, only enough for expenses, so that when the end of my engagement came, he told me to come into his office to collect. I had to go home for a suitcase to transport my pay from the club to the hotel. I did not have a handbag large enough to carry all the money.

When I got to Paris, I had to exchange my Greek money for gold in order to eat. I was happy to be back in my little hotel off the Champs Elysées, though most of my friends had gone away for the summer and had not returned as yet. I spent most of my days on the terrace of my room.

One of the first people I saw after my return was B. B. He and I had gradually drifted away from each other. We did not see one another for long periods at a time until at last nothing of our relationship remained.

I left for London a few days later to finish my last European engagement before going back to America.

A phone call had come from London asking, "What are you doing in Paris? We are expecting you here."

"I'm waiting for my work permit," was my answer.

"Who's taking care of it?"

"Foster Agency. Don't worry about it," I said. "Harry Foster will see that I get there before the opening date."

I had one week before my opening so I could take my time about getting there. I went by train, then took a boat that landed two hours from the city of London by car. Friends were supposed to meet me. So I waited on a hard bench for one hour before I heard American voices, singing and laughing, coming up the corridor of the building in which I sat.

When I walked outside, there stood a grand Rolls-Royce, chauffeur included. "See what we think of you? We drove all the way from London to meet you." I was proud to have such good friends and felt delighted, until I got the bill a week later.

4

While I had made no definite plans about America, I knew that I could now go home any time I wanted. Ed Robbins, a friend of mine with whom I had gone to school, had become a William Morris representative. He had been keeping in touch with me, asking me to let him know when I would be free to come to New York. A number of clubs were interested because of my European reputation, which was being talked about by Americans who had seen me perform.

A few days after I closed in London, I caught a plane to Paris. From there I was planning to take the *Queen Elizabeth* ten days later. My money had dwindled down to almost nothing, what with paying everyone else's expenses. Paris this time was rather lonely for me, though I did have some wonderful times with Michel de Merbe. We had met in Madrid, one night several years before. We became very good friends. When I arrived in New York, I had no place to stay, and since hotels were expensive, I called my old friend Roxie, who said, "Come on home. We are waiting for you."

The next day or so I had an audition at La Vie en Rose, where I met the William Morris representatives, along with Monte Proser, who wanted to give me a contract. The agency made the arrangements. Opening date was to be the eleventh of December, 1951.

Now another problem was presented because all my Parisian gowns had been more less used to a frazzle and I needed new ones. Roxie offered to make them.

During this period there was a strip running in the New York paper to advertise a "new sensation," first time in America. "Learn to say Eartha Kitt," the ad said. This ran for a period of ten days, up to the opening day, with the print getting larger every day. The idea that I was going to work in New York on my own home grounds frightened the bejesus out of me. I was in a complete daze from the day the contract was signed until—well, I still am, as a matter of fact.

Gradually I became aware of the awareness of me on the part of the public. People were saying, "What is this Eartha Kitt? I never heard of it before. Is it a liquor? Or a product of some kind?" There was also a notion that it was a Continental singer, who "doesn't know one word of English." All these comments came back to me. It made me numb to think that people were expecting something so "different."

During a rehearsal one day at the club, Mr. Proser asked, "How many languages can you sing in?" My answer was seven. "Then sing in seven languages," he said. As a result my program was made up of German, Spanish, Turkish, French, African, English, and Italian songs. As I ran through my songs with a Cuban drummer and the club's trio, people kept saying, "Be sexy, Kitty, be sexy." Sexy meant pelvic movements of all sorts.

Mr. Proser was staging me, somebody else planned the choreography, and the agents were telling me how to sing. Between them my act was programmed. I followed orders, too scared not to, for all of them must know what an American audience wanted, I thought.

My opening night arrived. The room was packed. My nerves were shot, and I was really too numb to feel anything. I don't even remember coming from upstairs, where my dressing room was, to the stage. The room was dark as I walked on to the dimly lit stage.

"This will prove if you are any good or not," my mind talked to me. The proof of the puddin' is to be successful at home.

I remember a blonde sitting at the ringside. Her reaction pinched my senses as each song started. Her expression changed as my songs changed. She leaned back in her chair with an expressionless face. As another language came up, she slumped. Still another, she folded her arms. Another, she looked at the man who sat with her. When I started my Turkish song, she shrugged her shoulders. My English song took her by surprise, and the German one made her exclaim, "Now really!"

I knew I was a flop before I went into my last song which was Afro-Cuban. I felt like a Christian being fed to the lions. I walked off stage after my one and only bow. I wanted to cry but I could not find a strong enough reason to. I think I was too scared to show anyone that I knew.

I wouldn't feel sorry for myself until I was alone. A few friends came in. "How wonderful you were!"

"Why do they say that?" I thought.

Roxie came in and sat in a chair without a word. Just smiled. Virginia Wicks, who was the publicity girl for me, came in. She stood on the side without a word. I had met her casually before this night, but she impressed me. She did not compliment or ridicule. She gave me the impression that she was aware of something being wrong. The problem was to find the cause.

After my room was emptied of the few who came to see me, Roxie said, "You weren't you, Kitty." I knew what she meant, but how could I find myself? I was too scared and confused to know who was me anymore.

I was petrified at the thought of having to do a second show. I almost prayed for something dreadful to happen to me, anything to prevent this torture. But I made up my mind it had to be done. I almost hypnotized myself into unconsciousness. I knew where I was, what my purpose was, how I had to go about it; but I refused to accept it.

I went on stage in a complete semiconscious state. One can will one's self into anything if the desire is strong enough. I was too ashamed to face a public and, most of all, those who had hired me, those who had had so much hope in me. Great expectations. How could I have failed them? My performance in the second show was a little better because I was not really there. Therefore I was more relaxed, but still it was not what I was capable of doing.

I went downstairs into the club after the last performance to meet some of the celebrities who had come to see an advertised sensation.

Judy Garland: How warm she was to talk to! How comforting her words were! "You'll be all right. You are afraid now, but you will find your way."

Artie Shaw, who was at the same table: "You have something. I don't know what it is, but you've got it."

Kay Thompson also gave me encouragement that night. "Look for your own path," she said.

I accepted the fact that I was a flop. I didn't read the papers to find out how much of a flop. The fact I knew. The degree was of minor importance.

For the next five days I went through absolute torture, trying to fulfill my obligations. Whenever I was alone, I felt the fangs of self-pity. No home to call my own—no mother—no money—and a flop. What can I do? Everyone in New York. knows I'm not a success. Who will give me a job? Oh, well, back to the factories, I suppose. I can't even go back to Paris, knowing I'm no good. How can I get up in front of an audience now?

Each night I went to work as though I was blindfolded. I saw nothing, felt nothing—except "not belonging." The only reason I was not fired was because no one wanted to hurt my feelings. My conscious mind wanted to stick out the two weeks, but my subconscious opposed it. I was ashamed to look the owners in the face. As a result, I never saw them. I'm sure they were there, all the time, but in my eyes they were not.

I went downstairs to do my show, as usual, in a highly nervous state. Miserably alone and filled with self-pity. All my songs went along, until the last. I haven't the faintest idea what happened. I found myself getting up off the floor. I scrambled to my feet still singing. I finished the show with needles sticking in my heart.

The gods were punishing me, I thought. This is not my medium, show business. I never want to see it again. Off stage, I sat down, too emotional to cry.

The producer came to me.

"How do you feel?"

"I can't describe how I feel."

"Well, you better do something about that chin."

"Chin? What about my chin?" I felt my face. A piece of flesh was hanging, dripping blood on to my white satin gown. A feeling of horror struck me. I did not realize how much of my chin was torn.

A feeling of joy struck me at the same time too. This might be a way out.

Then guilt, that old-fashioned guilt. I had done this deliberately in order to escape. How could one fall directly forward without a reflex of some kind to protect himself? How could my face hit the floor without some other part of my body hitting first? This I never figured out but secretly I knew why. Now a feeling of cowardice crept in. I was taken to the hospital within the hour, where I lay on a table and had six stitches taken in my chin. I watched the doctor put three needles in my face to deaden the tissue which he was going to sew. He threaded the needle and did his surgery while I watched.

Eddie and the stage producer waited in another room. When I came out about a half hour later, they laughed to keep me in good spirits. "Can you work tomorrow?" Eddie asked.

"I'll try," was my answer.

The next night, I removed the bandage, put my make-up on over the hanging stitches and went on stage. My mouth could open only so far because of the swelling and the pain, but I did my shows. Two days later my contract was cancelled.

5

Wallowing in self-pity, I stalked the streets of New York day after day. Strolling along Broadway I stopped at each display of cars. Cadillacs, Cadillacs, Cadillacs. A picture came into my mind. I was driving through Harlem in a white car with black upholstery, a mink stole thrown over one shoulder, all my friends piled in the back, laughing with happiness and prosperity. My dreams lost me in hopes, desires, and wishes. Eating bananas on my front porch while the sun shone gloriously on high.

My hair was straggly as I stood almost with my nose pressing the windowpane. I was a hungry little girl and inside the window all kinds of goodies made my mouth water.

My dungarees did not add much finish to me, nor did my shabby jacket, but my dreams took me completely away from this world into fairyland. In the reflection of the window I saw a man coming toward me, my Prince Charming. . . .

"This man doesn't know me," I thought. "Please don't let him know me."

He came nearer. This must still be a part of my dream.

"Please, no, please, please."

"Miss Eartha Kitt?" the voice asked.

"Ye—yes," I stammered.

I looked at him but avoided his eyes. I didn't want him to know how embarrassed I was. The face was recognizable but I could not place it. Out of my past came this face.

"My name is José Ferrer."

"Please don't be José Ferrer," my thoughts went on. "Not with me like this and a failure."

"I want to tell you how much I enjoy your work. I saw you at La Vie en Rose. You were wonderful."

"Th—thank you. I was not as I would have liked to have been, Mr. Ferrer—" I mumbled, "but I am glad I managed to please you, if I did at all."

"Which way are you going?"

"Uptown."

"I'll walk you to Fifty-ninth Street."

We walked along casually, talking casually.

He did not know that suddenly he had given me new hope. Maybe I was not as bad as I thought. Maybe I should pull myself together and prove that I am not a coward, after all.

Not long after this I got a call one day from Virginia Wicks, who asked me if I would be interested in working at the Village Vanguard. "It's not La Vie en Rose," she said, "but I thought you might be interested. It's up to you."

I couldn't say anything for a moment because I had to let it seep into my brain gradually that someone was interested enough to help me. "Have you spoken to them?"

"Yes. Max Gordon remembers you from the days of Dunham and is willing to give you a contract for two weeks, with options."

I got all my songs together to take down for a rehearsal. At the rehearsals, no one was allowed in the room. The trio and I went through songs they and I knew, ones I thought would go well, including some of my regular European repertoire. We wound up with almost the same program I had given in Paris and London. The songs for which I had no arrangements the trio wrote out for me or played by ear. I was very grateful to them for they gave me a lot of encouragement and made me work the way they played.

My opening night was a nervous one, as usual. The boys from the agency were there. There I stood on stage, again, hoping again to be loved.

The little room, holding about two hundred people, was warm and welcoming. The magnetism from my body went out in search of consolation and came back with the steady beat of my heart saying, "Love, love, love."

My engagement that was to be two weeks lengthened into fourteen, four of which were with John Carradine. The newspapers began to take notice of me again, and so I was able to pay my bills. My earnings were three hundred a week, out of which I paid Virginia thirty dollars to handle my publicity, which was a bargain, because she was entitled to much more. I knew that her regular fee for publicity was in the hundreds, but for some reason or the other Ginny felt I was not as bad as I was made out to be.

I was getting more popular. One day I received a letter from Leonard Sillman, whom I had never heard of, to call him on Tuesday to make an appointment as he would like to talk with me.

I called Charlie Baker of the agency. "Will you please call Mr. Sillman and tell him I can't make it today? Make another appointment."

Mr. Sillman asked me to come to a backers' audition of *New Faces of 1952*.

I walked on the dimly lit stage with so much fear I acted as though I knew only too well what I was doing. The truth of the matter was I was too insecure to look or act it. My defenses came up to protect me. But I was sure I had gotten through to someone. Obviously I did, because the debate on the contract started.

I went into the rehearsals of *New Faces* with sixteen other new faces, against everyone's suggestion. "I have a feeling," I said. "I can only follow it."

One day in the theater, the choreography for my part came up. We stood for three hours that afternoon, while various experts wondered what to do with me.

"Let's hear you sing the song again," they'd say.

"I met a rather amusing fool . . ." June Carroll's lyrics; Arthur Siegel's music.

At the end of the day nothing was accomplished.

That evening I went up to Mr. Sillman's apartment to talk about what I should do and rehearse with Arthur. "Why don't we use six chaise longues for that number?" I said to Mr. Sillman. "Let me crawl from couch to couch."

"That's a good idea," said Sillman.

The next day the chaise longue idea was introduced and it struck the experts completely dumb. When they finally came to realize that they were there to do my settings and choreography they got six chairs and spread them across the stage. It was then planned that I was to run to a couch, settle into a position awkward for singing, go through about three lines, then run downstage, sing a word or two to the audience—run to another couch, get into a reclining attitude, sing again—run, sing, recline, sing—run, sing, run.

The audience would never hear the song completely and I would be worn out by the time the curtain went down.

I rehearsed it this way, with the feeling that it was all wrong. I didn't want to change anything because I did not feel I was in a position to argue a point that I could not prove. It just seemed illogical that so much should go on during the actual singing. In between, when the music took over, yes. Otherwise the words were lost.

My costume was a pair of toreador pants and a black halter. For my French number, which was just walking across stage, more pants and another halter. I wore a dress in the opening and finale.

We opened in Philadelphia. Our notices were excellent. Mine were good, but I couldn't afford to be good. I had to be better than good.

At the party that night, everyone was happy about themselves except me. I got next to Mr. Sillman when he was feeling mellow.

"I want my spot changed, please."

"What do you mean? You did a wonderful job."

"I'm capable of doing better."

I had made a verbal bet with him that the way my spot was arranged, it would not stop the show.

"Oh, yes, it will," he had said. "You just wait and see."

I waited and I saw. It did not stop the show.

"I would like it changed, please, the way I want it."

"You'll stop the show in New York, don't worry."

"I want to be sure. Please change it."

"Okay, okay."

When we returned to New York to open after two weeks in the City of Brotherly Love, we took three days to work out the rough spots, including restaging my number. John Murray Anderson, who was our director, watched me work on my number. It was changed completely into what I wanted. As a matter of fact, I took over myself and did the choreography with some of the experts approving every move.

Opening night it did stop the show.

Afterwards a party was given for us in the Metropolitan Opera House ballroom by Mr. Chrysler, who was our main backer. All were waiting for the reviews. I wondered what we would have done had they been different from what they were. The show was a hit, and I was singled out as one of its most promising personalities: "Weird," "Strange," "Who can make a song burst into flame," "Feline," and so on. I had proved to myself, if no one else, that I was capable.

I went home that night thinking about my next venture. The Blue Angel. I was to open there the coming week.

6

My engagement at the Blue Angel was a successful one. I changed my repertoire a bit, got new gowns, and gained more security. The room held about two hundred people. Every night was Saturday night. I found myself crawling in on hands and knees because the front was the one and only entrance.

I had just enough time to go from the theater on the West Side to the club on the East Side, get dressed, and walk on stage. If it rained, I was usually late. Herb Jacoby would beat the entrance, pacing back and forth.

"Where have you been?" was my greeting for twenty-five weeks.

Now that my life had reached a leveling, I looked for an apartment to call a home. I found one through a friend who knew some boys who were moving out. When I went to see them, I was given details on how to go about the matter because certain people had never lived in the building before. "Maybe you will not have any trouble, but just in case . . ." They gave me the name of the housing commission and somebody else I was to call—just in case.

The boys helped me move my luggage into the three-room apartment on the ground floor.

"Just act as if you were our guest for a while. Say we are away. You don't know when we will be back." The boys left. I had paid them for the furniture, which was a studio bed, a chair, and nothing. I slept in the empty apartment until I could arrange to buy furniture.

About two weeks after I had made myself at home, someone knocked on my door about eight in the morning. It couldn't have been anyone but the landlord. I went sleepily to the door. Might as well get it over with.

"Who are you?" he asked.

I told him.

"What are you doing here?"

"I'm a guest."

"Where are the boys?"

"Away."

"When will they be back?"

"I don't know."

"How come *you* are staying here?"

"I had no place to stay, so the boys loaned me their place."

"Do you intend to keep this place?"

"I wish I could. I have been trying to find a place for months, but no luck. You know how difficult it is these days."

"Well, if you intend to keep this apartment, you're mistaken. There are some buildings in New York that do not allow Negroes in and this is one of them."

I looked him in the eye. He felt a little uneasy. I had the impression he didn't really want to say those words, but the words had to be said. "I'll give you a week to find another place." He walked out.

I thought of calling people but this might aggravate the situation. One cannot force his way into a world and be tolerated. He must make himself wanted.

Then too the landlord had the right to throw me out. In order to sublease, the owner should be notified.

I stayed on.

He came back about a week later.

"Well, have you found a place?"

"No, sir. I've tried but there isn't an empty apartment in New York."

"Why don't you try to find a place up in Harlem?"

"Why shouldn't I be allowed to live anywhere I please if I can afford it?" He stood against the living-room wall. "Would you like to be refused a decent place to live in for no other reason than the color of your skin?" I offered him a glass of milk. He accepted. "You and I are more or less in the same boat," I said, thinking of his last name. "You and I have a lot in common. You many more generations than I have. It's a pity to fight each other, don't you think?"

He drank his milk and moved in a softer mood. "You must find some other place. If anyone asks what you are doing in the building, say you are a maid." He closed the door and left.

I didn't expect that to come out of him. It struck me unaware. But I held on. Don't weaken your own will, weaken his. He can't be so terrible as all that. He wouldn't have accepted that glass of milk or have listened to you. I must handle this myself. If I win, so much the better. If I lose, at least I haven't created any more hatred.

A few days later he came back, with a soft knock on the door. "So you're still here, eh?"

"Yes."

"Were you thinking of staying here indefinitely?" I didn't know if he was trying to trap me or not, so I said nothing. "Would you like to have this apartment?"

Still not knowing, I said, "Well, this isn't the greatest apartment in the world."

"What's wrong with it?"

"The ceiling in the kitchen is torn. The pipes in the bath- room are rusty and they leak."

"I'll get all that done for you. Not only that, we'll paint the place, clean the floors, give you a nice comfortable place to live in as long as you insist."

Still not taking any chances, I said, "That's very nice, but to whom are you going to give the lease?"

"Here's your lease for two years. Sign here."

I read it and signed it.

I wondered what had changed his mind. He didn't know who or what I was until three months later, when he came and offered me the penthouse that I lived in for four years, with all the cooperation one can expect from a landlord, even to the paint. When later someone in the building asked him why was I living there, his answer was, "She has as much right as you to live anywhere she can afford. As far as we know, she's a wonderful girl and deserves it."

The Blue Angel brought me many happy moments. One night as I was leaving, the maître d' stopped me.

"There is a young man over there who is longing to meet you." He pointed to a table next to the wall. I glanced at him. "He has been in every night for ten days with the request to meet you."

"He looks so young. Should he be drinking?" I asked.

The maître d' laughed. "Please go over and say hello. He's a very nice boy. He's wonderful to us. We know him very well, he comes here very often." I didn't want to go because I wanted to get home. I was afraid he would get me in a conversation, making it difficult to break away. "He's always alone. Orders the same drink every night. He sees both shows, comes into the bar, sits down, waits until you leave, then he leaves."

"All right, I'll meet him."

"Miss Kitt . . . Mr. J. B."

"Hello," he said.

"Hi."

"I like your work."

"Thank you."

"Uh, I'm putting on a show sometime soon."

"Yes?"

"I wanted to meet you to ask you if you would be interested." He looked awfully young. "It's a, uh, musical. Would you be?"

I sensed a lie. "You can talk to my agents about it."

"Oh, who are they?"

"William Morris."

"I know them. How can I get in touch with you personally about it?"

"Through them." He was awfully young. "Good night," I said.

"Good night," he said softly.

I took a cab home as usual. The following night, he was there, sitting at a front table. I said hello, with a smile. He nodded back. On my way out, he sat in the usual place in the bar. I nodded good night. He smiled.

For several nights this scene took place until the maître d' came to me again. "You aren't being very nice to our friend. Why don't you have a drink or something with him? We think he's very lonely. It won't hurt you to sit for a while."

I went over. He got up to greet me. "You should know my act backwards by now," I said.

"I do." We both laughed. I ordered spaghetti. He ordered champagne. I ate heartily because the Blue Angel has good spaghetti. He drank heartily because seemingly he was lonely, although there was no sign of him weakening when the bottle was consumed.

"May I take you home?" he asked.

"I suppose."

He escorted me to an expensive car stationed in front of the club. He drove me to my door with small talk. When I bade him good night at the door, he said, "I'll meet you at three in the afternoon. Okay?"

"Okay."

The following day at three, sure enough, he rang my doorbell. I was in the process of hanging curtains, moving furniture, and so forth. He entered and immediately started to help.

"I have something to do downtown. Would you like to come along? I won't be long." We jumped into his car and were downtown in a jiffy. Madison Avenue at Fifty-something street. We parked the car around the corner from the jewelry store into which we went. The owner was introduced to me.

"Let me see something unusual," said J. B.

The owner brought out some antique pieces and laid them on the counter. I didn't pay too much attention because I knew I could not afford anything of the kind, so I half watched.

"Which piece do you like?" he asked.

"He must want me to help him pick a gift for someone," I thought. The piece I chose was a ring holding a large pearl with a cluster of sixteen diamonds around it. The price tag said one thousand dollars.

"Shall I wrap it up?" asked the owner.

"No, give it to her as it is." I was mute. J. B. smiled and said, "It's yours."

I was too surprised to say "thank you." Words were inadequate. J. B. led me out of the store in a daze, put me in the car, and drove me home.

"Now why would you wanna do a thing like that?" I finally asked.

"Maybe because I know what kind of life you've had and I like you," he said. "You are a great artist, whom I appreciate," he went on. "I want to make you happy. I don't want you to want for anything." Those words made me ill inside with content. Whether he meant them or not, I wanted to believe that someone really wanted to make me happy.

J. B. met me every night at the club to take me home. Sometimes he came over to help with the apartment. Soon we were inseparable. Every week he bought me a new piece of jewelry or added a piece of furniture to the apartment. He was gentle, considerate. Never had I met a boy so wonderful as he.

He gave me gifts of all kinds. In no time it seemed I had a completely new wardrobe, including minks that I never dreamed of owning at my age.

One night in the theater, Ronnie Graham and I got into a conversation. "How do you like my friend J. B.?" asked Ronnie.

"He's a wonderful person," I said.

"You sure know how to pick 'em."

"What do you mean by that?"

"He just inherited something like eight million dollars about six months ago." How many shocks can one have in a lifetime? "He belongs to one of America's richest families," Ronnie went on.

"I knew he was well off, but eight million . . ."

Our play ran for one year in New York. I remained in the Blue Angel six months of the twelve. J. B. was with me the whole time. He escorted me everywhere. For the first time in my life I had the security a woman looks for in a man. I suppose I began to depend on him for everything. A laugh, a sigh, good or bad, it was J. B. Every move I made was connected with J. B. I began to fear that awful world called society, rationalizing my way around it.

He was everything I thought I could want in a man. "Don't worry," he had said. "I can handle myself in any situation." My fears began to work on me. Could and would I ever belong to that society I feared so much, the world he belonged to that I had only touched the fringes of? I don't think either of us allowed ourselves to think of the consequences too much. We were too busy enjoying what we had and what we meant to each other.

Once in a while the subject came up, but J. B. always assured me he knew what he had gotten himself into. He had a mind of his own. I thought he was intelligent, witty, with his self-assurance. I was reprimanded by the Negro press for my relationship in a "downtown" world, and we both were slightly scorned by the downtown press for not conforming to society.

When I closed at the Blue Angel, J. B. met me at the theater. Sundays were our days together when no one could interrupt. We stayed in my apartment all day, reading, talking, or watching TV. We laughed heartily at each other's jokes, played as playfully as children. Each day became more enjoyable, until our Sundays became separable.

"I can't be with you this Sunday," he said.

"Why not?"

"I must have dinner with the family."

After that week, J. B. and I were never the same. We saw less and less of each other, which I never understood thoroughly, but in a few weeks for some reason or other J. B. went abroad, where he stayed for quite a while, never really coming back to me.

No, J. B. never really came back. When he returned I saw him once. He said something like—"Whether I love you or not has nothing to do with it. We cannot be as we have been." I was broken up to the point that everyone in the company moved closer to me in order to ease me. Virginia called constantly to console me. She talked to me for hours at a time to make me realize this was just one of those things. I must go forward, not sit and feel sorry for me. Everyone in life has disappointments. I was not the only one.

I wondered many hours of the days if I was not grieving for the Santa Claus he had been and I had never known before. Had I destroyed it or had society been too much for him to take? I felt unwanted, unpretty, uncharming, unattractive, uneverything. The one who had been everything to me was not there anymore. My pride—my dear, dear pride. Woman, thy name is vanity.

7

A few weeks later our show went on the road. Boston was our first stop.

About this time I made some records for RCA Victor that boosted my name a little further than it would have gone ordinarily. "Uska Dara" was the first single. This is where the real trouble with my obligations to Broadway began as far as *New Faces* was concerned.

My contract was for the run of the play in New York, with an increase in salary up to a certain point every six weeks. Now a renegotiation was called for. "You must be with the show," I was told. "The Shuberts won't give us a theater without you," was the word. "Three weeks in Boston. Four weeks in Chicago and we close."

"Then I can plan on a month's vacation before I begin nightclub singing," I thought.

Our three weeks in Boston were a cinch, but our four weeks in Chicago turned into eight months.

Charlie Morrison kept calling me about my contract with him, for by this time I had signed to appear in his Mocambo Club in Hollywood as soon as *New Faces* closed.

"I can't come until the show closes," I said.

"You have no business with the show now. You have outgrown that show," I was told.

"But I can't leave this unless I can't help myself. There are too many who say they depend on me." "C'est Si Bon" had come out while we were in Chicago. Now my name was a password. I was getting all kinds of offers. "I can't leave the show in midstream."

"When will the show close?" I would ask the management.

"In about a month," was always the answer. But "in a month" never seemed to come. As a result, my club engagements were cancelled about five times.

It was in Chicago I really began to have the taste of fame. I went to the beach with some friends one afternoon, as normal as normal is considered, lay back to worship the sun, as is usual in the summer. My eyes were closed, I was calm, thankful for serenity, with nothing on my mind but peace. "Is your name Ertie Kitt?" a tiny voice pounded faintly in my ear.

"Ertie Kitt?" I thought. She can't mean me. I opened my eyes to be sure.

"Are you the girl that sings 'Uskudidledadum'?" I couldn't think of what she meant for a second. Then I heard laughter. I had forgotten that I had even made a record, except for "Monotonous," which was in the *New Faces* album.

"You mean, Usku dara gederikin?" I said when I stopped laughing.

The kids that were around me began to laugh again. "Sing a little bit for us?" one asked. I felt very silly but sang a phrase or so, thinking this would satisfy them. They ran off.

I went back into my peace mood. A few minutes passed. "May I have your autograph?" And the tiny voice was in my ear. I opened my eyes to see a little boy with six other little boys, holding a piece of brown paper. They had ripped up an old paper bag.

"What does that say?" one boy asked.

"That's my name."

"But I can't read it." We all laughed. "Sing us some of the songs?"

"I can't. I'm not supposed to do this for nothing." I tried to get out of it.

"You sang it for them." I was trapped. I wound up singing "Uska Dara" five times before I realized the only thing to do was leave, as a crowd had gathered. Some had seen the show. Some had heard the "strange record," as they called it. Some wanted to know if the language was real or was it make-believe. "What kind of language is that?" I was asked. "How did you learn such a strange tongue?" "Were you in Turkey?" "How did you get there?" "Where is Turkey?" "Are they our ally or our enemy?"

Every day that I went to the beach thereafter was spent in signing autographs or giving a lecture on Turkey.

Club offers were more insistent now. "You've fulfilled your obligation. No one can ask you to give more than you have. You can be making big money now."

This I knew, but my conscience would never have forgiven me if I "deserted" the kids. The clubs kept calling the agency and I kept putting the dates off. Our producer kept saying we were going to close and I became more of a public figure as time went by. I began to hear my records played on juke boxes as well as on the radio. Disc jockeys began to talk about the new up-and-coming songbird.

At first the strangeness of hearing my own voice out of the air fascinated me. I had accomplished something. The longing for my mother became stronger. I wanted her to share in my success. Now I could afford to give her all the things to make a mother happy. She wouldn't have to work anymore. I could take care of her. Maybe eventually . . . buy a house with a front porch and eat bananas all day! I wondered often why both my aunt and mother were taken away before I could make their lives comfortable.

"C'est Si Bon," people would say when they saw me walking down the street or into a restaurant. I felt wanted. I was getting the love I had always wanted, though the love was in a different form than the love of mother and daughter or father. I was getting it the hard way, for I had to constantly prove myself in order to maintain it. It was a kind of love one could not take for granted.

When my recording company began to talk to me about making hit records, I said, "I don't want to be an artist who has to live on his latest record. This does not prove I'm an artist, only that I am being advertised, like Coca-Cola. What happens to me when I don't have a hit?" I explained that I must be the artist I thought I was capable of being. If I happened to have a hit record in this process, so much the better. They understood my point of view, which made my relationship with RCA Victor and Henri René a very healthy one. Besides, we have learned that albums are security, like annuities. A single record serves to make one popular fast, makes money fast, but can die fast.

Our eight months in Chicago finally ended, and the show was on the way to Hollywood to film. A few days before leaving, I got a call from Charlie Morrison about doubling into the Mocambo.

"That would be very difficult, Charlie," I said. "Our studio call will be in the wee morning hours."

"You can do it," he said. "I need you." It was wonderful to have someone say "I need you." "I would like to have you for three weeks. You'll be here for that amount of time."

"I don't know, Charlie."

"Please, Eartha. You don't know what this will mean to me."

I knew Charlie Morrison to be a very honest and considerate person. His reputation was the best, and I was never a good one for saying no when asked a favor.

"Okay, Charlie, I'll see what I can do."

My contract was up with *New Faces* again. Our producer told me the show had been offered three weeks in San Francisco and two weeks in Los Angeles and asked if I would stay on for those five weeks.

"Five weeks?" I said.

"Yes. Five."

"You told me we would be through after Broadway. Then two weeks in Boston, four in Chicago. We have been in Chicago for eight months. Now the movie. . . ."

"You have to do the movie anyway. They won't do this picture without you," he said. I didn't really believe this, though I had heard it before. How much did they really depend on me? I could not figure out. Anyway, just in case they did depend on me more than I thought they did, I decided not to take a chance, for the sake of everyone concerned, mainly myself, because I did not want to lose the love the company had for me.

I had had to hire a secretary the last month in Chicago because my fan mail had piled up and I could not catch up with it by myself. Other activities kept me too busy. I sent my secretary on to Hollywood three days before we left Chicago to make various arrangements, hotel, publicity for the club, and disc jockey promotions under the supervision from Virginia Wicks' office in New York. Rennie got a cabin of two bedrooms, living room, kitchen, and bath at the Garden of Allah on Sunset Boulevard. When I arrived, flowers greeted me in every part of the house, making me feel welcome.

Rennie and I went to the Mocambo for dinner, where we met Mrs. Morrison and the people of the club. A few days later we started shooting the film in the Western Studio lot. The call was for eight A.M. A few days later I opened at the Mocambo. My call was from ten-thirty P.M. until twelve-thirty A.M.

When I drove up to the club the first night, I saw a huge banner stretching from one side of the Boulevard to the other, directly in front of the Mocambo. I paid no attention to it until Rennie said, "Now really!"

"What?"

"Look at that." The biggest letters you have ever seen in an advertisement said: **EARTHA KITT**. The marquee said the same thing.

If I was nervous before, you can imagine the jitters I got after that. I couldn't even put my make-up on properly. I kept drinking hot coffee, tea, water, anything hot to calm my nerves. Nothing worked. I was all dressed and ready for the show to start when I got sick at my stomach. Charlie Morrison came down to console me. He had filled my room with champagne that complemented the flowers that covered my whole room. "Take a sip of brandy. It will calm you down."

I took the tiny glass and gulped it down, stinging my vocal cords to strangulation. I could hardly breathe when I stepped onto the tiny stage that was just wide enough for the mic and me.

The crowd looked at me. I looked at them, searching for a smile to comfort me. I found many. I looked from face to face, slowly, in order to get my equilibrium before starting. Applause went up to welcome me.

I was excited by the sensation going down my spine, for I had not expected such a welcome. I was new in the business. No one, I thought, knew me this well. I had only made a few records, sung a few clubs, and had been on Broadway all this time. How could anyone know me? (I forgot I had a good publicity office, too, to let everyone know I was around.)

The applause eased me a little as I went into my opening song. Arthur Siegel, who wrote the music for "Monotonous," accompanied me on the piano. I was glad he was so close because he was always good for a laugh, and he laughed constantly himself.

Whenever I was a little uncertain during the show, I looked at him. He would laugh, as though nothing mattered, and cheer me up. He never knew, until one day I told him, what a comfort it was to have him on the stage. When I told him, he laughed so hard he nearly strangled himself to death. After that, I never complimented him without a glass of water handy. "Really," he'd say, and off he'd go into laughter. He was a very serious young man.

"Santa Baby" was received with big yaks—so was "C'est Si Bon."

The more serious numbers, such as "Lilac Wine," written by James Shelton, were liked for the change of mood. When I left the stage, I was a "star," said Charlie Morrison.

The applause went on for an uncomfortable length of time.

"What do I do now?"

"Go back and sing some more."

"I don't have any more."

"You must have more songs."

"I only rehearsed ten with the orchestra."

"Doesn't your pianist know any?"

"To tell you the truth, I'm too scared to go back. I might spoil what I have created."

I went to my dressing room on the verge of tears. I was so happy to—whatever anyone might call it—it's to "belong." I felt it in the theater; yes, it was there, but here I was closer. I could see their faces, every smile, every expression of love.

If I can come this close to the border of world acceptance, can I go further? I went to my dressing room in love of the world. Why couldn't my mother or my aunt have seen this? Champagne flowed in my room, as friends and fans crowded in to congratulate me.

When all had left me in my dressing room for a breather before the second show, I sat down to take a cup of tea. I was tired, but I could not allow myself to be. Rennie sat with me, saying nothing, for she had grown used to my quiet moments. She refused visitors so I could rest for a while.

The second show went on. I forgot my fatigue and every saddened moment as I met my audience. I was a happy child when I went to my cabin that night.

I took a hot bath, to soak away the aches, to calm me down, to put me to sleep, but it was not that easy. I stayed awake, thinking about why people become what they become. The lack of what one does not have, such as bread and water—a mother or father—or just a drive to go forward? If that lack was not there, would there still be the same drive? How much of it is luck too?

If only I had someone to share this with, even if it only lasted a couple of months, I could have made my mother very happy. Having all this alone doesn't seem to be right, it doesn't fit properly.

At seven I went to the studio to be made up and get ready for call. I nodded in my studio cabin between my takes and someone else's. I had had only two songs alone in the Broadway show, but Eddy Alperson, our film producer, gave me five spots in the picture. He also had my wardrobe specially made. The film took us about ten days, with much confusion, because Broadway does not understand Hollywood, and Hollywood, of course, doesn't understand Broadway. Each knows what is good for itself but not for the other.

I felt very strange in front of a camera, because one's movement is restricted, but, all in all, I did not mind film making. After ten days, I was pretty worn out, even though a couple of those days I did not have to go into the studio.

I kept my sanity, though. Rennie's argument with me was that I would not eat. One day I'd eat well, the next day nothing at all. I had been that way ever since I can remember. Only when I'm hungry will I eat. Having to go without food when I was little may have set up a pattern, I suppose. An analyst would know. I wonder if this is why I have a habit of giving things away? My schoolteacher, Mrs. Banks, told me once, "You'll never have anything, Eartha, because you give everything away." Well, it's a joy to be able to give. Misers never seem to be very happy people.

Anyway, the banner hung across the street for ten days. Whenever I drove under it or saw it from a distance, a proudness came up in me, tinged with fear. That name really did not belong to me. It belonged to a friend of mine, someone I loved and wanted only the best for, someone for whom I'd want everything that I'd want for me. I had not yet obtained it, she had. There was no real connection with that name and me.

8

One night a group of stars was asked to do a benefit for Mayor Paulson, in honor of the King and Queen of Greece, at the Ambassador Hotel in Hollywood. The head of the committee came to see me to make arrangements.

"Which songs do you want me to sing?" I asked.

"Oh, 'C'est Si Bon,' 'Santa Baby,' or 'Evil'—anything you are known for would be fine," I was told.

"How many songs?"

"Two is what everyone else is doing, but be prepared for three or four."

Arthur and I went in the car that was sent for us. I wore a dress that covered all; even my neck was barely seen. We sat with June Allyson and Dick Powell. Dick made me feel less nervous. I don't know how he did it because he was just as nervous. "You don't have a thing to worry about," he said. "Just remember they are nervous too."

We all sat on pins and needles with sliding cushions. We kept glancing at the Queen, who is one of the most attractive women I have ever seen.

The dinner was over, the drum started its roll. Harry James came out to head the orchestra and Dick Powell walked up to the microphone, graciously acknowledging the royal couple to bring the meeting to order. He read a delightful poem to her majesty, which eased everyone. We all laughed our nervousness away.

I was the first to be introduced, because it was nearing my show time. Dick Powell has no idea what he did to me spiritually that night by the way he introduced me, because we have not seen each other since then, but he gave me a new kind of feeling. "One of our great artists, Miss Eartha Kitt."

June Allyson looked at me with the kind of warmth only she can give, which put me at ease. I sang my song, "I Want to Be Evil."

I was completely unprepared for the burst of applause. I had thought everyone would be a bit reserved because of our royal guests, but this was not the case.

I sang my second song, "Santa Baby." Again an outburst. But two songs should be enough, I thought, because everyone wanted to share in the ceremony of welcome to the King and Queen. I started back to my seat, but was applauded back to the microphone. I did Duke Ellington's "Blues"—and ended with "C'est Si Bon." The crowd came forth with laughter mingled with applause as I said good night to June, waved bye-bye to Dick, and fled the room to my paid audience waiting at the Mocambo.

That night I did my second show to a full house with standees. The streets were traffic jammed. And I was happy. A few days later, I called a rehearsal to put in some new numbers. I was standing in the middle of the stage when someone told me there was a phone call.

"Eartha, what did you do at the King and Queen's ball the other night?"

"What do you mean?"

"There was a meeting Tuesday at the mayor's office. You were called down as un-American."

"*What?*"

"The subject of the benefit came up. The mayor said you were not what should have been good American art. Can we come over and take pictures?"

"What have I done? I only did what I was told to do."

"Well, the mayor thinks you are risqué."

"Risqué?" I was speechless. "What is this all about?"

Even before I left the rehearsal, several photographers had come in to photograph what the mayor had called risqué. For several days headlines made everyone on the West Coast conscious of Eartha Kitt as a result of this little episode.

Mr. Rio, head of the American Guild of Variety Artists, came to the rescue. "If this is the way an artist is treated after a benefit performance, no more benefits," he said. "We contributed a million dollars' worth of talent and they call us names."

Hollywood backed us up. "The mayor obviously does not know what American is." "What does he mean by risqué?" "Invite the mayor to see the show, Eartha."

Which we did, but he never showed up. The feud went on for days.

I was on the spot and in the spotlight. My record sales went sky-high.

I got a contract from El Rancho at Las Vegas for ten thousand dollars a week, a million dollars' worth of free publicity, and found a million friends.

Hollywood was really wonderful to me during that episode. I am especially grateful to Mr. Jack Benny, who had a long talk with the mayor at a dinner of some kind a few days later and seemingly put him right. The only bad effect of the incident was the letters I got, including one which came to me a year later on Broadway: "There is nothing more enticing than a Guthrie McClintic production, but I shall refrain from coming to see yours because of your vulgar display before the King and Queen." But one wonderful thing put everything in its proper place. It was the telegram from the royal couple, saying, "We don't know what all the fuss is about. We thoroughly enjoyed the show."

During my engagement at the Mocambo, Charlie Morrison swarmed me with gifts of appreciation, to the point that I wanted to cry—and did closing night.

Every day there was something new in my cabin. A cashmere sweater with mink cuffs—a cashmere sweater with fox—a hat—a scarf—a bottle of champagne—a bottle of perfume—flowers—something.

I remember Charlie coming into my cabin with a bucket of champagne on ice, a bottle of wine under his arm, followed by two waiters, one with a turkey as big as I was, the other with a tray at least a yard long, covered with autumn leaves and heaped with grapes painted gold, all sorts of fruit, orchids on long stems, ears of corn of many colors, and whatnot. It was the most beautiful thing I had ever seen. I wouldn't let anyone touch the fruit in it for days.

For some months I had been under a doctor's care. I had been told by a medic in Chicago that I was anemic, that my blood count was ridiculously low. "I don't understand why you are not in bed," he said. "You are a walking corpse."

I was given all kinds of iron tablets, liver injections, and a list of foods to eat. I had to be examined twice a week or so. I was to remain as calm as possible, even take a vacation if I could. I continued treatments in Los Angeles to keep going. By the end of my stay in Los Angeles, I was too tired to do anything, but I had to go on.

A needle was put into my arm on the average of every other day for six months, vitamins, liver, iron, calcium, to keep me on my feet. Every time I felt exhausted, I got another needle in my arm to pep me up. I understood why some people turned to alcohol or dope or anything, just to keep going.

I got depressed very easily because I was tired. I had always been moody but not to this extent. However, on the Tuesday night of my last week at the Mocambo, I was feeling my usual self. The company of *New Faces* was there, and we were all sitting upstairs with Mr. and Mrs. Charlie Morrison. My eyes glanced up to see a pale, worn, warm face coming in the door. His eyes glanced directly at mine. The time was right, the face was right, and the man. . . .

"Who's that boy standing in the door?" I asked Mary.

"Oh, that's . . ." She never finished her sentence because Charlie went to greet him. The two of them came over to our table. The pale-faced boy sat down and ordered a drink. He was introduced by his first name. I got up because Frank had come to tell me it was show time. The paleface grabbed my arm.

"Don't go away," he said.

"I have to. I have to get dressed."

"Come back."

"I have to come back up to work," I said.

"I mean here. Come back and have a drink with me." He held fast to my arm.

"I'll come back," I said. During my songs I saw him sitting by himself at a long table. Mary and Charlie had left because it was late.

When I returned to my dressing room downstairs, the pale-face came in. "I didn't think you'd come back so I came down to be sure." I smiled. We went to have hamburgers and coffee. "I've been waiting a long time to meet you," he said. I was silent, wondering how much he meant by these words. He took me home after a while. "Don't go to bed," he said. "Stay and talk with me."

"I'm tired."

"Well, I'm going to stay right here."

I was too tired to argue with him, so I went off to bed. When I woke up the next morning, he was asleep on the sofa in the living room. He left for home after having coffee but came back to pick me up that afternoon. For the remaining seven days of my engagement we were inseparable.

A few days before we left for San Francisco, he gave me my first birthday party at the Mocambo. When I arrived at the club, all our mutual friends were sitting at the large table set up for the birthday dinner. Flowers were arranged majestically in the center; a place was left empty at the head of it for me. A tiny box topped by a bouquet lay next to my place. I opened it nervously. The tiniest angel riding on three clouds that were tiny fresh-water pearls looked up at me

The card said, "You may want to be evil, but I think you are an angel."

Well, nothing much will come of this anyway, I thought. When I leave town, that will be the end. A day or so later we opened in San Francisco. The evening of our arrival he called. I was happy to be missed. Every day for the first week or so he called.

"I'll be over on the weekend." The weekend arrived; he was there. We did up the town. Ronnie Graham, some other members of the company, the producer, and I went with him to call on Hoagy Carmichael. I never laughed more in my life listening to two funny men play on words the way he and Ronnie did. My paleface was always good for a laugh. He was warm, he was lovable, he was kind, but he was lonely. I felt the longing for someone to talk to. He was always laughing at himself. I never knew a more wonderful sense of humor.

I was at ease with him. I learned through him that, though our lives were completely different, I was the lucky one. I had everything in life to reach for, to fight for, to hope for, to want. He had no place to go. He hung from a chandelier over a table of desserts. He was lonely, so was I. The time was right, the place was right, when I returned to Hollywood, the man was right.

"I went all through Switzerland with your voice haunting me on the radio," he said. "I made up my mind to look you up when I got home. What could have been more surprising than to look down the hill and see the name I had been looking for?" We went everywhere together. Parties and places. Our friends were wonderful to us. We were happy. We were doing our Broadway show in a downtown Hollywood theater.

Charlie Morrison asked me again if I would double at the Mocambo. "It will be too difficult, Charlie, especially on matinee days." But it was impossible to say no to him, remembering how wonderful he had been to me.

My first closing at the club had been one an entertainer never forgets. Charlie came downstairs before the first show that last night and gave me a pounded-gold cigarette case with my name on it. A diamond dotted the i. Before the last show he came down and gave me a gold medallion of the Virgin of Guadaloupe, the Virgin of Mercy, to protect me in time of need.

My heart was swollen with emotion when I went on stage. After my first three songs a line of waiters came up on stage and presented me with many bouquets of roses. I was so overcome with happiness I looked at Arthur at the piano for consolation. Not knowing what else to do, he started to giggle, which tipped the buckets of tears in my eyes so that they rolled down my cheeks.

I put my flowers on the piano, flicked my fingers across my eyes in order not to show my tears, and started my song. I got choked, and the tears rolled. The audience was silent.

Then applause started. I cried some more. The audience sniffled. Handkerchiefs were being taken from handbags.

The music started again. I wiped my eyes, and then I laughed. The audience laughed. I turned my back, composed myself, and continued my show. How could I say no when Charlie asked me for another three weeks?

Every night after the theater curtain went down, I dashed into the wings to remove my costume, slipped into my pants and overcoat. The car was waiting for me. We flew across Los Angeles to arrive just in time for me to slip on my evening gown and walk on stage.

The crowds were about the same as before. The weather was bad for a spell. It rained, which made it difficult because I caught a virus. One matinee I was too weak to walk, too sick to sit, too stubborn to lie down, and too hoarse to sing. My doctor came. "You have a bad infection and should be in bed."

I did half the show and was sent home. Every half hour I was regurgitating. I was given a sedative, which put me to sleep. I did not go to the Mocambo that night either. "The rest will do you good," the doctor said.

Charlie Morrison was very understanding, but the newspapers said, "Eartha Kitt's walkout on *New Faces* gained her no friends." Another said, "We don't mind anyone trying to make money while the making is good, but Miss Kitt should realize she has seventeen other kids to think about."

I had been told that the show would close after Hollywood, but our producer came to me with the proposition that we could go back to San Francisco for five weeks and tour back to New York. "You said you were closing," I pointed out.

"I know that, but business has been very good. We can go on for a little while longer if you are with us."

"I've made other commitments because I expected this to be over long before now." I was told if I left there would be no tour. "I'm awfully tired," I said. "Besides, my engagements are overlapping each other. Buffalo says they will not let me out of my contract again."

I didn't think it wise to return to San Francisco but everyone else disagreed. Since I did not want to be blamed for perhaps being responsible for closing the show and putting others out of work, I consented to tour except for the eight days I had to be in Buffalo. We opened again in the City of Seven Hills and I left for Buffalo some days later.

Business was fine for those days. We had two weeks off between San Francisco and the next engagement, when I again returned to the Mocambo. On April 1, 1954, the show closed on the road.

Our producer had offered to put my name on the marquee, but I refused this because I thought it would be unfair to the rest. We had started out as a family; we should wind up that way. If the public chose to pick a favorite, that was their doing.

My paleface continued to call me regularly wherever I was. "When are you coming home?" was his main concern.

9

April 7, 1954, I opened at El Rancho Vegas in Las Vegas, Nevada. I remember when I got off the plane in the desert, a member of the hotel staff was there to meet me with my secretary, who had gone ahead to make preparations. Driving from the airport to the highway, I saw a sign advertising the star who was to appear at the El Rancho. Letters taller than I spelled a name that I could not make a complete identification with—**EARTHA KITT**.

When we reached the hotel, a sign on each side of the road said the same thing. Someone who had something to do with me had become a headliner. I was taken to my cabin of luxury that was just like a regular little house, everything included. A bottle of champagne waited in a bucket. Flowers scented my room. I felt strange and alone, but wanted.

My rehearsal was the same afternoon I arrived. Bill Loose, whom I asked to accompany me at Henri René's suggestion, took over the orchestra with the arrangements he had made for me. He knew my work because he had done some of the arrangements for me at RCA. The guitarist that Bill had found for me was also there to ease the way.

Mr. Katleman, El Rancho's boss, came into the rehearsal to greet me. During the middle of a song. he came across the room saying, "Hello, there." I looked at him and continued the song to the end before saying "Hello." Beldon Katleman and I got along famously from the first moment because, as one of the orchestra men said, "You are two of a kind. When you like you like, and when you don't, there's no pretending."

My engagement was successful, thank heavens, as Buffalo had been. Champagne was in my room every night for the two weeks. Mr. Katleman proved himself a friend and a gentleman and I have never met a nicer wife or hostess than Millie.

A few days after we were there, my paleface came down to meet me. No one was happier than I because everything was going so well. Since *New Faces* had closed, a new play, *Mrs. Patterson*, was being prepared for me by the same producer. "Don't get entangled," I was told by some. This was something new for me in America. Although I had proclaimed myself an actress in Europe, I had become popular in my own country as a singer of songs. "Don't press your luck too far," they were saying. "Be satisfied with what you are." "You are making a good living as a club artist. Why fool around with it?" I would think about it.

I continued to fulfill my engagements in the nightclubs, including the Latin Casino in Philadelphia, where I worked for two of the nicest persons in the club world, Dave Dushoff and Dave Dallas. Boston, and finally New York, La Vie en Rose. My fears there were more acute than at any other time because of the bad experience at the beginning of my career in America. I had been trying to avoid it for some time, although I knew better than to let a bad experience get the better of me. It was like getting back on a horse after he had thrown you.

When I finally agreed to the offer, I felt I had been made conscious enough of the American public to have a bit more confidence, so I went ahead. I walked out on the stage of La Vie en Rose as though I had not a fear or a care in the world, but my insides burned. The room was packed to the brim, for which I was grateful, and after the first three songs, my fears were forgotten because the audience was with me, seemingly, all the way.

Happiness hugged my breast when I walked off stage to encore applause, for I had conquered my own defeat. New York, the Empire State, had built my little empire inside of me. I was happy to be a part of such a tumultuous world that can destroy so quickly and build just as fast.

My publicist, Virginia Wicks, by this time had become my Rock of Gibraltar. I have not said much about Virginia, mainly because there are no words to describe what she has meant to me as a person, let alone publicist, and one whom I have chosen for my friend. I say chosen, and that in itself is the greatest compliment. Families are tied by many knots, but when a friend is chosen it is because of her consideration and warm understanding. Virginia has stuck by me when I thought there was no shoulder to lean on.

My tears, my fears, my joys, my success have all been shared by her, and I hope she stays with me till the end. She was once described by Chris O'Donnell as a hard-working, painstaking creature during the day who changes into complete femininity after six.

After an engagement at Lake Tahoe, the Cal-Neva Club, I drove to Hollywood through the most beautiful park I had ever been in. I drove for eleven hours through beauty and serenity. The roads were rough and narrow and the height was frightening as my Ford climbed to the ceiling of an enchanting world.

When I arrived in Hollywood, my paleface greeted me with, "At last." The discussion as to when I would leave was our main topic, as I was on my way to do the Broadway show. I was not too happy about the commitment, for I wanted to be with him. The idea that I would be in the show for no telling how long sorrowed me. But I had made up my mind to do what I thought was right, for the sake of what was expected of me. I was now a star of the cabarets, which was the public's doing. At this early stage of the game, I did not think it correct to think only of my own needs and desires. There was too much to be done.

I remembered the phrases of some of the people who came to see me. "You are a great credit to the race." "You are an asset to Americanism." "We are depending on you." "Truly a great artist. . . ."

I wanted to stay in California. "You are never here," my paleface said. "Three months away, two weeks here. Why don't you get an apartment?" We began to make plans for my moving to California after the closing of *Mrs. Patterson*.

When I reached New York and went into rehearsals of the show, I became conscious of the difference between the world of the cabarets and that of the legitimate theater. The play was directed by Guthrie McClintic, who left me absolutely alone to create as I wished.

"She can't play a fifteen-year-old. She's too sophisticated," the word went around. I knew what my capabilities were, but it was difficult to convince others of this. Everyone can give advice after one is successful, but no one can tell you how it comes about. The end of rehearsal evenings found me worn to a frazzle, for the emotional involvements of the part took everything out of me.

It took me back to the South that I held no remorse for leaving, back to a world I had to recognize, but which I kept peeling off as though it was dead skin. The fear that one day I might again eat the same bread to sop up the same molasses turned into a benevolent brother and stimulated my soul to create again what I had once experienced. All this was unconsciously eating away my energy, helped by fatigue and nervous tension.

I spent all day with the others on the stage, crawling on the floor, crying with my character, laughing, giggling, forgetting I was the nightclub personality who had made ten thousand dollars a week at El Rancho. My one consolation in my depressed state was my paleface's phone calls twice a week.

When the show opened in Detroit, it got fair reviews. Me? By all the angels that guide me, which I will always believe is the spirit of my mother, I was safe. My personal reviews were wonderful, but because of the not-so-good notices of the play as a whole, we worked on it every day for the three or four weeks we were in

Detroit. One morning I was awakened by the phone at four A.M. I faintly heard my paleface saying, "Hello, Earthie."

"What's the matter? Are you ill?" I asked.

"No."

"Why do you call me at this hour?" I said, though I was glad to hear his voice.

"I want to tell you something." He could hardly be heard. I was sure something was wrong. I waited, pressing the phone closer to my ear fearfully, hoping I would hear right. "If I tell you something will you remember it tomorrow?"

"Why . . . yes, what . . .is . . .it?" stilled my breathing. The walls were silent, the air in my room crept by sympathetically.

"I love you!" The words hugged my ears, possessed my heart, closed my eyes, and smoothed my brow to love. My lips could not make a sound to destroy this beauty. I held the phone, not wanting to interrupt the glow that suddenly hung slightly overhead.

"You're drunk," I said, laughing.

"Yes, I am. If not, I probably would not be able to tell you, but I have loved you for a long time, afraid to reveal how I felt."

"Why didn't you tell me when I was there?"

"I didn't know how to. It was easier to say nothing."

"You won't remember this tomorrow. You're too drunk," I teased him.

"I know what I'm saying and I will say the same thing tomorrow."

"All right, call me tomorrow. If you tell me the same thing then, I will believe you, providing you are not drunk again."

I could not go back to sleep for some time after the call, and I went to the theater that evening in the best of spirits. My performance was better than ever, I thought, for my creative powers were more sensitively alive.

When I returned to my hotel, I expected some message from my paleface but he had not called as he had said he would. Three days later, after I had convinced myself he didn't mean to tell me what he did, he called. "Yes, I love you," was the phrase I wanted to hear as it came three thousand miles.

"What do we do now?" I asked.

"I don't know," he said. "I have never been in this situation before. I love you but I will never be able to marry you." I understood what he meant, although I was unhappy about it. Even so, with all the aggravations of our relationship, we planned to have me move to where he was after my play closed. I would get a house or an apartment so that we could at least be near each other. I would arrange my club engagements so that I would be at home a great deal of the time. I was not satisfied with this by a long shot, but we were in love. To be in love meant sacrifices or doing what we thought would make us happy for as long as we saw fit, or as society allowed us. Society did not allow us to follow our plans, for our relationship was soon cheapened by slanderous improvisations.

For the two months that our show was in Chicago, where again the play was criticized but I was on safe ground, I was happy. I went nowhere, saw no one, stayed in my room with my books, counting the days to be with him, although I knew not when it could be. Besides, most of the time I was too tired to even walk around my room. Then my throat had become irritated during rehearsals and never did come back to normal. Each day I thought maybe it would today, but it remained the same. This was the beginning of a horrible siege, even though beauty halfway bowed her head to me at every turn. Later my throat had to be operated on because of overwork, but that's another story.

Mrs. Patterson opened in New York to a glorious house. When I came on stage, applause welcomed me. "You must leave Eartha Kitt in the wings when you go on," I had said to myself.

My room was so filled with flowers they could not all fit in my two dressing rooms. I had received one hundred and twelve telegrams of good wishes, including some which called me "one of the greats of our time."

Could I live up to it? The stage floor was a stage of thin ice for me to tread. To hold my own or to sink through and die, never to be remembered. I sensed the presence of the critics in the first couple of rows. I did not find my bearings mentally until the third act, when I really tore myself apart. "You don't have to be so realistic," my favorite stage manager, Morty Helphurn, had said to me. "Take it easy, don't give so much. You'll wear yourself out."

When the final curtain went down, I went droopingly to my dressing rooms in the Broadway theater on Forty-first Street. I was about to take my make-up off when the doors began to open. A line had formed that went through one dressing room and out the other. "You were great!" said a voice. "You were magnificent." You were this, you were that, went through me. Some were still crying from the last act.

Morty opened the champagne that had been sent by Bob Collins, a friend. I was toasted, I was greeted, I was hugged, I was kissed, I was happy, but there was no one to share it with. Virginia stood on the side, smiling with happiness for me. She understood what was going on inside of me. These were the times I wished for my mother or aunt.

The crowd went on forever, until I was happily exhausted. Then came the letdown. I put my head in my hands and I cried. The show party was some distance away. When we arrived, mostly everyone was there. We waited nervously until the papers came out. I don't think I heard clearly any of the words of the reviews exactly. I do remember everyone kept saying, "The greatest reviews of the year."

I was numb, I heard nothing. I saw very little, I felt less. I was too tired and, I suppose, excited to absorb anything. "You should be a very happy young lady," Ginnie said. But I did not realize what she meant until three or four days later when I went to the theater and saw the printed signs of what the critics had said about me. Not really me but Eartha Kitt, for I felt less connected with her now than at any other time. But it seemed really true that Eartha Kitt had become a star.

Printed in the USA
CPSIA information can be obtained
at www.ICGtesting.com
LVHW010306231123
764760LV00030B/297

9 781958 425282